Delta Primer

Delta Primer
a field guide to the California Delta
with a preface by Kevin Starr

Jane Wolff

William Stout Publishers, San Francisco

William Stout Publishers
530 Greenwich Street
San Francisco, CA 94133

Distributed in North America by
RAM Publications and Distribution
2525 Michigan Avenue, A2
Santa Monica, CA 90404
310.453.0043
310.264.4888
rampub@gte.net

The publication of this book was made possible by funding from the
Graham Foundation for Advanced Studies in the Fine Arts, the LEF
Foundation, and the Great Valley Center.
Delta Primer would not have been undertaken without a seed grant
from the California College of Arts and Crafts, and it could not
have been finished without the generous support of the Ohio State
University.

ISBN 0-9709731-6-0 (paperback)
ISBN 0-9709731-7-9 (hardcover)

Library of Congress Control Number: 2003107768

Printed in China by Palace Press International.

Contents

Preface

Thinking about water is a complicated activity. Thinking about water in California can approach higher mathematics in complexity; for contemporary California invented itself through water engineering; and the intricacies and effects, intended or otherwise, of that invention are multiple. Thinking about the California Delta only compounds the problem, for this eco-region sustains within itself every positive and negative legacy of the way that Americans have re-structured the environment since seizing California from Mexico in 1846. In *Delta Primer* Jane Wolff penetrates the maze with deceptive simplicity. Both in terms of its method and its message, this breakthrough study advances, simultaneously, the cause of the Delta, hence the cause of the overall environment of California, and the methodology of environmental science itself.

From Aristotle onwards, philosophers have always sought to distinguish—which is to say, to separate, to deconstruct—in order to unite. The proper object of analysis, then, is to re-unite complexity into larger patterns that can, in turn, be used as a basis for action. The mere deconstruction of a problem into its component parts most often results in paralysis. Action demands re-integration of complexity or, if total re-integration proves impossible, then at least an acknowledgement of resistant problems and/or necessary trade-offs.

In *Delta Primer* Jane Wolff offers readers the issues and tools of analysis and action. She does this traditionally with photographs, an historical essay, and a vocabulary of useful terms. With brilliant simplicity, she also adds a fourth approach: an inventory of the Delta as garden, wilderness, machine, and toy, all this organized as a deck of playing cards. Each card is a map of one or another Delta value and/or characteristic and belongs to a garden, wilderness, machine, or toy suite. Wolff has thus inventoried the Delta from the 1850s to the present into its component parts. But she has not left these parts in isolation from each other. The reader is invited, rather, to combine or separate characteristics as one would assemble or re-assemble playing cards in various combinations seeking a winning hand. Thus the reader—and, one hopes, generations of environmentalists to come—can use the cards of the Delta Primer to determine which characteristics and values are compatible with each other and which elements are incompatible, inconsistent, or intractable and hence must be traded off or left behind.

The *Delta Primer* is hence a toolkit and a kit of parts that represents, I believe, a breakthrough in the methodology of environmental science. Open-ended, flexible, multiple and comprehensive, Wolff's primer invites us, in effect, to a charrette. She does not, however, determine the outcome, nor does she lock anyone into rigid categories or lines of action. By avoiding the one hundred percent solution, moreover, she invites as many different types of people, values, and outlooks as possible into the game. From this perspective, Delta Primer is scrupulously non-partisan within its environmentalists' orientation. Politics, Aristotle tells us—even environmental politics—is the art of the possible, and Jane Wolff knows that while no solution is perfect, more than one solution can be possible.

California has need of the *Delta Primer* not only for the saving of the Delta itself but also for the case study that saving the Delta, if and when the Delta is saved, would offer the rest of the state. By 2040, many predict, there could be as many as sixty million people in California. (Wolff prefers the more cautious figure of fifty million by 2030.) Dealing with this growth is the great public business of our time. If we can understand and hence better serve the Delta, Wolff's primer suggests, then perhaps we can come to a better understanding of, and a better program for, the inevitable growth faced by California.

In Wolff's scenario, the Delta—like California itself—is a product of nature, time, choice, action, and technology. Here converge the two great rivers of the state, the Sacramento and the San Joaquin, seeking release in the Pacific; but here as well there would be only an inland sea, a watery wilderness, had not human beings engineered another alternative. In the nineteenth century, great levees, many of them built by the Chinese, disciplined the meandering waters of the Delta into channels. From this channeling emerged a paradox: as contained waters rose behind their levees, the rescued lands began to sink below sea level, transforming the Delta into a Holland-like landscape. Until the 1880s, the waters and lands of the Delta were abused by the sediment of hydraulic mining, but this was stopped by legal action, and the Delta was developed into abundant fields of potatoes and pear orchards. In the 1930s a deep-water channel was cut through the region, transforming the city of Stockton into an inland port. Now great sea-going ships could cross the Delta, seeming, from a distance, to be gliding across the land, through the pear orchards, like lost leviathans. In the second half of the twentieth century, the drainage basin of the San Joaquin Valley, the Delta, became as well a source of water for a developing Southern California. More channels and two great aqueducts were built, and these in turn had their effect on the land forms and water courses of the region. The very fish of the Delta became transients, taken from collection points and transported by tank trucks past the dangers of pumping stations. Two super highways, meanwhile, California 80 and Interstate 5 sealed the Delta into isolation but also facilitated its encirclement by encroaching suburbs. Did these suburbs constitute a wall of protection, or were their grids already crisscrossing the region, dividing and sub-dividing into sections soon to be developed?

Land, water, agriculture, technology, a rising tide of suburban sprawl–the Delta had it all by the year 2003, and so did California. But like California as well, the Delta also called to pleasure and the joy of life. It was a recreational area of almost representative quality: a place to lie in wait for ducks in a blind on a cold and foggy morning, or laze in the sun on the deck of one's Boxie Boat, a houseboat peculiar to the region. The very garden identity of the Delta enhanced its capacity to give pleasure. Here was more than nature. Here was nature improved by art, while in the background, always and everywhere, was Mount Diablo, rising over the Delta, Wolff tells us, like Mount Fuji in a Japanese painting, a sublime presence in a garden of delight, reminding one and all that even in nature tamed by the garden, nature always has the last word.

While blessed by nature, then, the Delta was not the product of nature alone. It was the product of nature shaped by human action, as was most of California by the end of the twentieth century. In the case of both the Delta and California as a whole, each adjustment, each intervention, had intended or unintended consequences. These side effects, in turn, became the premises of new processes and identities.

The growth, finally, that is being predicted–fifty million by 2030 as Wolff argues, sixty million by 2040 as others claim–is engendering a deep malaise among Californians. Can Californians manage such growth creatively and in an environmentally responsible manner? Can what is left of natural California be preserved in the face of these predicted densities? Jane Wolff does not answer such questions. She does, however, give us the analytical elements and tools with which such questions can be answered in terms of the Delta and, by implication, in terms of California as a whole. She also provides us with pathways of history and value that are equally useful.

The Delta, as Jane Wolff tells the story, was from the beginning a respected, even cherished, place. With the exception of the dumping of hydraulic sediment, catastrophic violence to the Delta was kept to a minimum in the nineteenth century. Well through the first half of the twentieth century, in fact, the Delta was preserved through agriculture as a managed garden. Although there were abuses, the Delta did not suffer the ravages of rampant industrialization. Indeed, there were even certain beneficial side effects, such as the newly created wetlands becoming a favored stopover to millions of birds migrating each year along the Pacific Flyway, thus transforming the Delta into one of the great bird sanctuaries of the continent, where even avid duck hunters align themselves with conservationists.

So, too, did the Delta, as Jane Wolff describes it, ever maintain its human dimension.

Here was a region, after all, that would not even exist, had no people brought it into existence. *Delta Primer* is careful to list and in many cases describe the first American settlers in the region, the people behind the names that now dot the islands, pockets, channels and wetlands. They were Native American names, Anglo-American names, African-American names, Asian-American names, Californians all, finding themselves in a distinctive environment and learning to cherish the land which they were wresting from the sea and from which they earned their living. Despite mistakes and losses, even the occasional bad behavior that expanding human settlement invariably brings in its wake, such affection for the Delta has persisted across the decades. The Delta has never lost its status as a bellwether place. In terms of the way that California has invented itself through water, here can be found—on the edge of the fourth largest metropolitan region in the United States—a compelling paradigm of both the power and the fragility of nature in California and the losses and gains intrinsic to development. While not formally listed in her deck of Delta cards, there is one card that Jane Wolff constantly plays and that is her informed and disciplined affection for the region. Not only is Jane Wolff helping us to understand the Delta and, by implication California, she is reminding us through the tribute of her comprehensive and caring scholarship that for environments to be saved, they must be understood, true, but also loved and cherished. Such deep affection—for the Delta, for California, for planet Earth—constitutes a card in its own suite. It is the one card we must all have—and play—in common.

Kevin Starr
State Librarian of California
Sacramento, California
June 2003

Sunflowers, near Cosumnes River, 2002

Potato sorter, Bacon Island, 2000

Flood damage, Egbert Tract, 1997

Cantina, Bacon Island, 1997

Communal garden, Locke, 2002

Weir, Delta Cross Channel, 2002

Japantown, Isleton, 1997

View from packing shed, Bacon Island, 2002

Orchard, Andrus Island, 1997

Paddock, Union Island, 1997

Middle River, 2002

A Brief History of the Delta

If you stood in the middle of one of the islands in the Sacramento-San Joaquin Delta, where the Great Central Valley of California drains into San Francisco Bay, you might not know that you were twenty feet below sea level. You might not realize that the rational agricultural geometry around you ended abruptly at the meandering river on the island's edge. You might not understand that the ditches running through the fields were dug for drainage rather than irrigation. You might not think that there was anything strange about the Delta until you saw an ocean-going freighter cruise by in the distance, eighty miles from the Golden Gate and fifteen feet above your head. If you climbed to the top of the levee that separates the island from the river, though, you would see land and water together, and then you might wonder how the landscape became such a paradox.

A History of Unexpected Consequences
In 1850 the Delta was still wild. A tidal marsh, it consisted of low-lying islands among the distributary channels of California's two great rivers, the Sacramento and the San Joaquin. It was a landscape in flux: river channels moved, water levels varied, and land flooded and dried out with changes in the seasons and the tides. The history of its dilemmas begins in that year, when Congress passed the Swamp and Overflowed Lands Act and made marshlands available for settlement on the condition that they were re-claimed for agriculture. The act specified small holdings and prohibited the resale of land. Claims were made, but reclamation at the scale of the small farm was difficult. After legal changes in the late 1860s ended the limits on parcel size and consolidation, groups of investors accumulated large tracts of land and undertook the Delta's wholesale reclamation.[1]

The early settlers built low levees around the islands to stop seasonal flooding, and they drained and cultivated the interiors. These interventions had an unforeseen result: the land began to sink. The region's peat soils were extremely fertile, but they were unstable. The peat oxidized when tilling exposed it to air, and it blew away as it dried out. The ground began to subside at a rate of several inches a year.

1 / California State Lands Commission, *Delta-Estuary: California's Inland Coast* (Sacramento: State of California, 1991), p. 67; see also John Thompson, *The Settlement Geography of the Sacramento-San Joaquin Delta, California* (doctoral dissertation, Stanford University, 1958), Appendix B.

2/Edward Dutra, "History of Sidedraft Clamshell Dredging in California" (Rio Vista, California: Dutra Dredging Company, 1976), p. 3.

3/Hydraulic mining was outlawed in 1884 because of its devastating effects on the Delta. For a discussion of this groundbreaking environmental policy, see Gray Brechin's *Imperial San Francisco: Urban Power, Earthly Ruin* (Berkeley: University of California Press, 1999).

To compensate, farmers made the levees higher and stronger. Starting in the late 19th century, they used the clamshell dredger, developed in the Delta, to move alluvial material from the river channels to the levees.[2] The fortification of the levees had its own unanticipated effect: the rivers began to rise. Because they eliminated the flood plain, the levees increased the volume of water in the river channels during the rainy season. The channels began to silt up with the alluvial sediment that had formerly replenished the surface of the islands, and the level of water in the rivers rose even when they weren't flooding. Hydraulic mining in the Sierra Nevada sent huge amounts of soil and rock into the Delta and made the channel bottoms still higher.[3] Flooding became a constant threat rather than a seasonal one.

As the scale of cultivation increased, the infrastructure needed to support it became more extreme. The land fell so low that groundwater had to be pumped up and out of the fields. Levees required constant repairs and additions to compensate for shrinkage, cracking, and damage caused by hydrostatic pressure. Engineering was not able to create stasis in the fluctuating systems of the Delta; each intervention had consequences that made new interventions necessary. The landscape became a hybrid of cultural intention and natural process, and the line between nature and artifice grew more and more difficult to draw.

The Multiplication of Complexity

The Delta is a rural landscape, but the transformation of its physical geography over the last 150 years has been closely connected to cities. Urban capital and urban markets drove reclamation and the subsidence it produced. Building levees was expensive, and many reclamation projects were funded by consortia of investors.[4] The large-scale land ownership needed to make reclamation feasible meant that the region was never characterized by subsistence agriculture. By the 1870s farming was being carried out at a commercial scale: early vegetables were sold in central California towns; peaches, pears, livestock, hay, and dairy products were sent to San Francisco; and after the completion of the transcontinental rail lines, fruit was exported to markets in the East.[5]

4/Thompson, *op.cit.*, Appendix B.

5/*ibid.*, p.310

By the late 19th century the economic agenda for the Delta had expanded, and the consequences of human intervention had multiplied. Commercial fisheries introduced striped bass and American shad in the 1870s and 1880s, and these exotic species began to compete with natives.[6] The transport of goods to market also complicated the region's ecology. Invasive species were inadvertently brought to the Delta in the ballast water of ships; since 1933, when the Stockton Deep Water Channel was completed, ocean-going boats carrying organisms from other ecosystems have been able to cruise as far as ninety miles inland from the Golden Gate.

After World War II, the Delta became the centerpiece of the infrastructure that supplies water to Southern California. The large-scale export of water from the Delta began in 1951, when the Delta-Mendota Canal opened. Funded by the Federal government, its purpose was to provide irrigation water for the Central Valley. An ancillary installation, the Delta Cross Channel, was built to carry water across the Delta and toward giant pumps that fed the canal. In 1973 the State of California opened another canal, the California Aqueduct, to take water from the Delta to Los Angeles and San Diego. It had its own pumping plant; next to the pumps, a new forebay allowed sediment to settle out of the water before it was sent to the south.

The export canals transformed the meaning of the Delta's rivers. They had been a local transportation system for farmers and produce, and they became the center of a giant plumbing network extending for hundreds of miles and serving distant constituencies. Water export changed the rivers' ecology, too. Sending vast amounts of water to the canals instead of the ocean allowed salt water from San Francisco Bay to migrate upstream. The force of the pumping changed the direction and quantity of water flow significantly enough to confuse the native fish that migrate through the region. Instead of swimming toward the ocean they went into the pumps, and their population began to decline dramatically.

Unlike the consequences of earlier interventions, the changes wrought by water export provoked conflict. Water export threatened the farmers in the Delta: salty water in the rivers would produce salty groundwater in the

6/California State Lands Commission, *op. cit.,* p.81.

soil, and land could quickly become unfit for cultivation. It also mobilized environmentalists, who were concerned about its devastating effects on native species.

The conflict produced new institutions and new management strategies. Local agencies were chartered in the Delta to negotiate with the Department of Water Resources about water quality. New measures were developed to protect endangered species. Enormous screens were installed to remove fish from the mouth of the pumps. A protocol was developed to identify, count, measure, and record the collected fish; to take them in specially-adapted tanker trucks across the Delta to a point just above the mouth of the Sacramento, out of reach of the pumps; and to put them back into the river. Even this well-organized, highly choreographed strategy has had unexpected consequences, though. The striped bass that were introduced for fishing follow the schedule and location of the fish drops. They wait for the trucks, and they eat the fish that have just been rescued from the pumps. So far nothing has been done about this development. Measures that could eliminate the exotic predators would also destroy the native species whose welfare is a legal mandate.

Disputed Territory
All of the powerful and conflicting forces that are shaping the California landscape today converge in the Delta: suburban development, environmental politics, the changing economics of agriculture, and the endless demand for water.

The range of people who want something from the Delta has grown to include local farmers; farmers in the Central Valley; ecologists and environmental activists; boaters, fishermen, windsurfers, birdwatchers, hunters, and other recreational users; suburban developers in the cities and towns that ring the Delta; and the inhabitants of Southern California. Their goals for the landscape are different; they understand it in different ways; and they imagine its future differently. The fault lines among the Delta's constituents are complicated, variable, and sometimes counterintuitive. They do not fall according to simple boundaries—urban interests against rural interests, for instance, or water exporters versus water conservers, or local constituencies against distant ones—and they shift from case to case.

One source of dissent is water use. Some groups depend on keeping as much water in the rivers as possible, and others want to maximize exports. Delta farmers need enough fresh water in the rivers to keep the salt water of San Francisco Bay out of the groundwater that runs through and below the land, and environmentalists and ecologists want sufficient flows to support native plant and animal species. On the other side, farmers in the San Joaquin Valley irrigate their crops using water from the Delta, and the expanding cities of Southern California demand more and more water, especially as their right to Colorado River supplies is challenged by states upstream.

Conflicts also arise over land use and management. Farmers in the Delta want to stay in business, but environmentalists propose to turn prime agricultural land into nature preserves, water engineers suggest flooding subsided islands to create reservoirs, and suburban developers are active all the way around the region's perimeter. Delta farmers and ecologists struggle with boaters and jet-skiers, but for different reasons. The wake from the boats and skis erodes the levees that the farmers must maintain, and the fuel additives emitted by two-stroke engines are harmful to flora and fauna. Such alliances shift with respect to different questions, though. For instance, farmers advocate the dredging of river channels to reduce flood hazards, but environmental legislation severely restricts dredging because it increases sediment in the water and harms fish.

In 1994, state and Federal agencies formed a consortium called CALFED to negotiate the Delta's contested future. CALFED's contradictory mandate is to meet the increasing demand for water in Southern California and to maintain and enhance environmental quality in the Delta. Its advisory board crosses the spectrum of groups with interests in the Delta: the Central Delta Water Agency, Ducks Unlimited, the Natural Resources Defense Council, the Paskenta Band of Nomlaki Indians, the United Farm Workers of America, the Pacific Coast Federation of Fishermen's Association, the

7/CALFED Bay-
Delta Program,
California Bay
Delta Public
Advisory
Committee,
http://www.
calfed.water.
ca.gov/bdpac/
BDPAC_
Members.html,
2/24/02.

8/This proposal
recalled the
the Peripheral
Canal, an
aqueduct
proposed in
the 1970's to
carry water
directly from
the Sacramento
River to the
pumps. The
canal would
have made it
possible to cut
off the water
supply to the
Delta. It was
the subject of a
state referendum
in 1982.
The majority
of the state's
population lived
in Southern
California, but
voter turnout
there was
low; turnout
in Northern
California was
high enough
to defeat the
proposal.

California Farm Bureau Federation, the City of West Sacramento, the Bay Institute, the Inland Empire Utilities Agency, the Kern County Water Agency, and the Metropolitan Water District of Southern California comprise only a partial list.[7]

CALFED has entertained a wide range of proposals. One was to flood subsided islands to make a reservoir and wetland system that would run through the middle of the Delta; another was to build a canal that would carry water around the edge of the Delta rather than through it.[8] It was impossible to reach consensus on the more radical strategies, and the group has decided on a program that simply makes adjustments to the current situation. No one's goals are truly satisfied. Local interests are concerned that limits have not been set for export, but water exporters believe that the system does not guarantee adequate supply. Chances are good that the current plan will change.

There is no end game in the Delta. The cost and difficulty of maintaining the region's infrastructure are only increasing. On the other hand, if the levees fail and the region is inundated, salt water from San Francisco Bay will migrate upstream. Giving up the struggle would mean losing things that society wants from the landscape: fertile agricultural land, the remnants of a unique ecosystem, and, not least, the water supply for nearly two thirds of California. Management is not a question, but how the landscape should be managed, and to what end, are fiercely contested topics. The outcome is likely to be determined through a public process.

New Nature?

In 1860 what people in cities wanted from the Delta was produce. In 1960 it was water. Today it is something less tangible: the illusion of nature. That illusion is being made by an improbable concurrence of interests: CALFED is offering funding for ecosystem restoration as a condition of water export, and so environmental groups have allied themselves with constituencies in the southern part of the state. In a certain way the alliance is not so strange. Like the increasing demand for water, the desire for nature is a product of urbanization. As cities expand, that longing becomes more urgent: the homogeneous suburban mat becomes more oppressive, and wild places (or even places that look wild) are harder and harder to find. The interest environmentalists have in protecting endangered fish is not exactly the same as the one that Los Angeles has in obtaining water, but like all of the positions advocated by the Delta's constituents, it assumes that people can and should determine an agenda for the landscape.

To make new nature, subsided land is taken out of agricultural production and native wetland plants are grown instead. CALFED is currently studying the purchase of one of the largest of these efforts, which will transform four very low-lying agricultural islands in the middle of the Delta. Two of the islands will become wetland areas and two will become reservoirs that can compensate for seasonal differences in the availability of water. Beyond that, new nature may help to make development at the Delta's perimeter possible: developers in nearby cities and suburbs have proposed to pay for wetlands projects in the Delta to fulfill legal requirements for environmental mitigation.

New nature does not imply freedom from human control. It depends completely on the levee system built to overcome wilderness: without the levees, the Delta's subsided islands would flood. Giving up control would make the Delta into a wild inland sea completely unlike the landscape that existed before reclamation.

It is possible to see unmanaged nature in the Delta. It exists at Franks Tract, a former island that was reclaimed for agriculture and cultivated until 1938.[9] That year the levee was breached and the land behind it flooded. Because the cost of repairing the breach and pumping the land dry again was prohibitive, the island remained inundated. Wind created waves strong enough to erode the levee from inside, where it was not reinforced, and it deteriorated into small fragments overgrown with cattails and tules. The island has become an open lake with enough erosive force to threaten the levees that protect neighboring farmland. Its agricultural past is under water, and the marshy ecosystem that preceded it is irrevocably lost.

9/Thompson, op. cit., p.464.

What Next?

There are 32 million people in California now. If the population continues to grow at its present rate there will be 50 million people in 2025. The more people there are, the more complicated their agendas for the Delta will be. The negotiation of their competing desires is likely to transform the landscape, and what happens will have a powerful effect on the economy and ecology of the whole state.

Most of the 20 million people who depend on the Delta today don't even know that it exists, and conventional planning is not educating them about what's at stake. There are many threats to the Delta's future, but the greatest one is its invisibility.

Delta Primer

The *Delta Primer* is intended as a political tool.

It arose from the conviction that mobilizing consciousness at a grassroots level is the first step toward effecting change. Its purpose is not to advocate a particular solution for the Delta but to ask people to look carefully at the landscape and its dilemmas; to propose that change can and should be informed by the richness and complexity of what already exists; and to suggest that multiple readings and uses of the place can go forward together.

The premise of the project is that documentary stories about the landscape, represented in ways that most people understand, might generate terms for thinking about the future. The *Delta Primer* tells those stories in different ways: as photographs, as a brief history, as a lexicon, and as a playing card map.

The playing card map was inspired by familiar objects: maps, which organize information about the landscape spatially, and playing cards, which provide a system for establishing and exchanging relative values. Maps and cards have had a relationship before. In the 16th and 17th centuries, maps of the fifty-two counties of England and Wales made the faces of the fifty-two cards in a standard deck.[10] Other decks represented the four continents as

10/Carl Moreland and David Bannister, *Antique Maps* (London: Phaidon Press, 1993), Chapter 9.

the four suits in the deck; the cards in each suit were the countries on each continent.[11]

The playing card map makes a new relationship between the composition of a map and the system of a card deck. The United States Geological Survey map of the Delta has been divided into sixty pieces. Each piece of the map is paired with a drawing about an artifact, practice, or process related to that place, and the drawing has been designed as the face of a playing card. In this book, the paired maps and drawings are presented on facing pages. If the drawings were printed on the opposite sides of the maps, the project's back would comprise a puzzle and its front would make up a deck of cards.

Just like an ordinary deck of cards, the deck has four suits and fifty-two ranked cards. The four suits represent four ideas about the Delta: that it is a garden, a wilderness, a machine, and a toy. These categories are broad; they are open to interpretation; they are outside the usual boundaries of the Delta's interest groups; and almost everyone with a stake in the Delta can see his or her interests in all four of them. Each card is assigned to a suit depending on its subject and ranked according to its scale. The bigger the scale of the story it tells, the higher the value. There are eight more cards: four wild cards make a panorama of what the Delta's future might be like, and four unranked cards comprise a map of the region.

The Delta is full of multiple readings, and some of the stories could have been put into more than one suit. In those cases, the most vivid slant on the story determined its category. In an ideal future every card would belong to every suit: every story (and every place on the map) could be understood in terms of all the themes that define the landscape.

The cards might be used to play gin rummy, or poker, or go fish, or hearts. None of these games is a bad metaphor for a negotiation about the Delta's future. The choice of one card (or story) is made at the expense of another; no one ever has all the cards; different combinations of cards produce solutions of equal worth; and what matters in the end is the definition of values, the system of exchange, and the willingness of the participants to play.

11/Multiple examples were collected by Lady Charlotte Schreiber in *Playing Cards of various Ages and Countries, Vols. I-III* (London: John Murray, 1893-95).

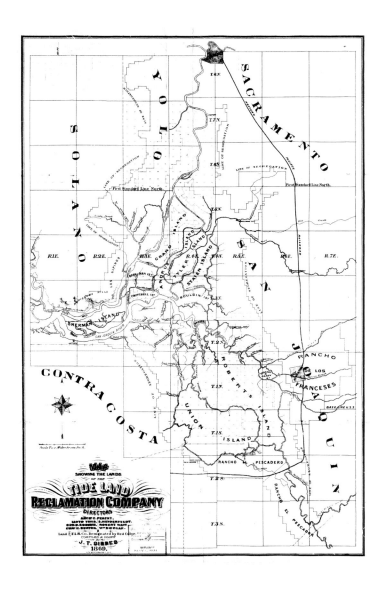

The Delta, 1869

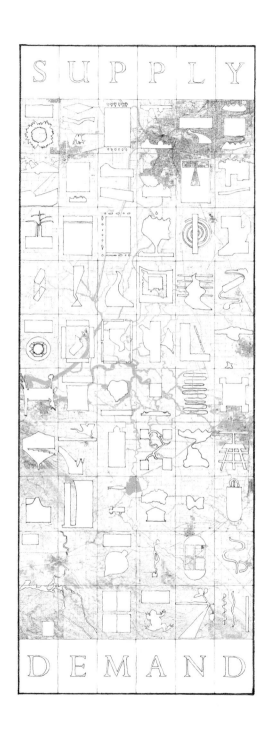

The Delta, 2002

The Livermore
Valley is an
inland place,
but the Bay
Area has
expanded to
include it.

Map 49   50

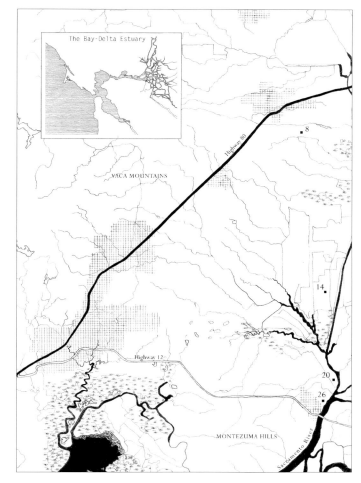

The Bay and the Delta comprise the largest tidal estuary on the West Coast.

The ecology of Suisun Marsh is different from the marshes in the Delta: west of the X-2 line, the water is substantially saltier.

The urban
growth along
Highway 580
marks the
southern edge
of the Delta.
Development
extends east of
Livermore to
Tracy. Bay
Area traffic
reports have
begun to
include the
Altamont Pass,
and there
is a new
commuter
train from
Stockton to
San Jose.

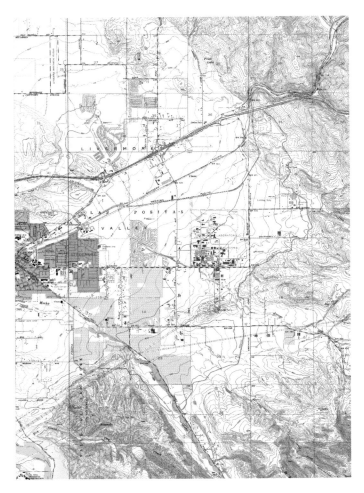

Map 50

52

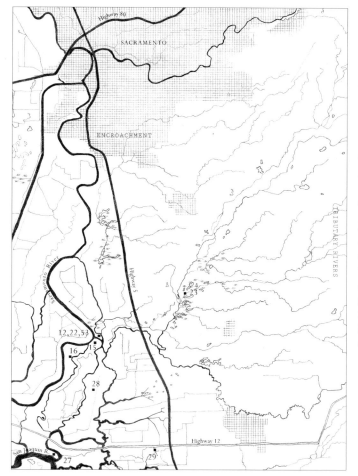

Highway 5, which connects Sacramento and Stockton, marks the east edge of the Delta.

The tributaries of the Sacramento and San Joaquin come together at the west side of the Great Valley. They are dispersed again in the Delta as the land flattens out.

The Delta: Northeast

San Francisco imports its water from the Sierra Nevada through the Hetch-Hetchy Aqueduct. No major city in California has enough local water to support its population: water is always being taken from somewhere else.

Map 55

54

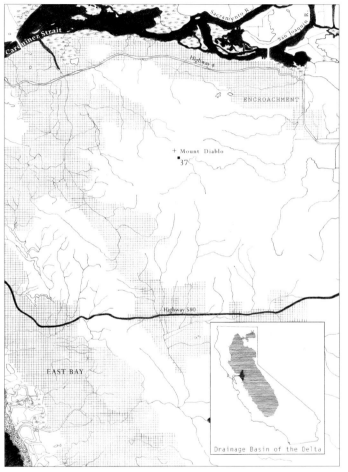

After the Sacramento and the San Joaquin converge, their water travels through the Carquinez Strait to San Francisco Bay.

All of the water in the Great Central Valley of California has one outlet to the Pacific: the Delta.

Lake del Valle
was built
by the
Department of
Water
Resources. It
feeds the South
Bay Aqueduct;
the water goes
to Santa Clara
and Alameda
Counties.

The hills that
separate the
Delta from the
bay are largely
uninhabited, but their protection means that
development leapfrogs to the next valley.

Map 56   56

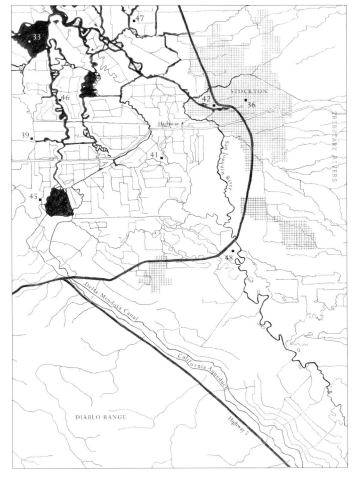

The San
Joaquin River
carries less
water
than the
Sacramento:
its drainage
basin is drier,
and there are
more
diversions
upstream.

The rivers
carry water
into the Delta,
and the
acqueducts
take it away.

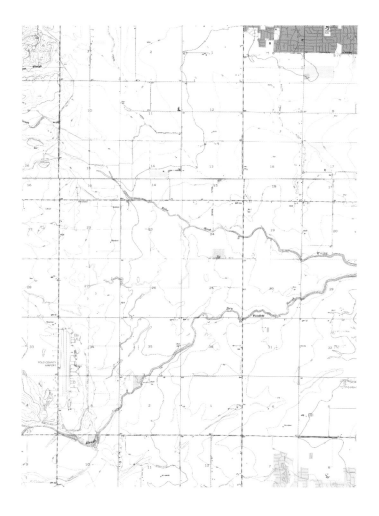

Map 1   58

Garden is the set of artifacts and practices that relate to inhabiting and cultivating the landscape. It is manifest not only in the fields that farmers till but also in the suburbs where people dream of a life between nature and the city.

Asparagus was first grown in the Delta in 1852. It became one of the region's main crops. In 1929, there were ten canneries between Walnut Grove and Rio Vista. Isleton became the center of the Delta's canning industry. Asparagus was shipped all over by train and boat: in the early 20th century the Delta produced 90% of the world's asparagus.

Map 13   60

2

A S P A R A G U S

People in the
Delta call
asparagus
grass.

Asparagus is
still harvested
by hand. The
shoots are cut
from below
the ground
with a special
knife, tied into
bundles, and
collected in
small carts.

A The peat soils of the Delta are suited to asparagus.
B Root stock has a productive life of up to 20 years.
C Roots are buried in a shallow trench.
D Soil is mounded against the growing shoots.
E One stalk emerges from the root at a time.
F When a stalk is harvested the root sends up another.
G The last stalk of the season is allowed to mature.

2

Unlike most
row crops,
asparagus is more visible after the harvest than before. During the growing season
the plants' shoots are cut before they produce leaves, and the fields look bare.
After the last cutting of the year the plants leaf out and the fields turn green.

Pears are the main tree crop in the Delta. There are about 6000 acres of orchards in production, and about 120,000 tons of pears are harvested every year.

Pear trees need high ground. They will not tolerate the soggy conditions in the bowls of the islands.

The pear year begins in March, when the trees bloom. During the

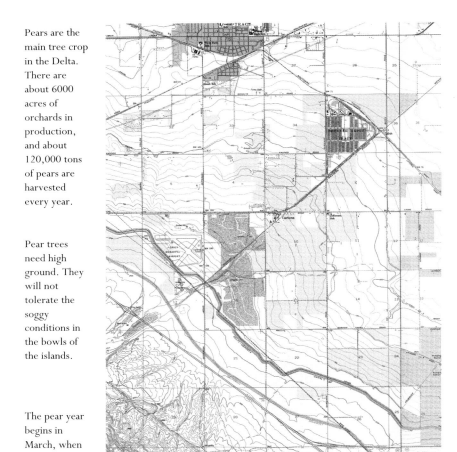

growing season all the orchards must be irrigated and sprayed for disease and pests. The harvest usually lasts from July through August. In the autumn the trees are pruned.

Map 53   62

3

PRUNING   WEEDING

PICKING   TRANSPORT

Mr. Wong's day

Mr. Wong Yow lived in Locke and worked in the orchards near Walnut Grove. He kept a diary with exhaustive notes about how he spent his time.

Mr. Wong's year, showing hours worked per month

The diary is a record of the physical labor of cultivation: weeding, irrigating, pruning, transporting fruit, cutting blighted branches, transporting blighted branches, repairing crates, repairing ladders, transporting crates, transporting ladders, dumping garbage, cutting trees, aerating soil, and keeping watch at night.

The Delta is full of the romance of decay: roads warp, the ground falls away from buildings, renegade sunflowers grow through cracks in pavement.

The kitchen garden is south of Courtland, on Tyler Island. It sits at the edge of one of the orchards that line the Sacramento River and its distributary channels.

Map 15   64

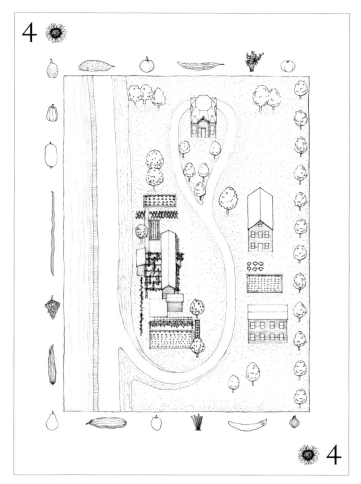

This kitchen garden, tended by pear growers of Chinese descent, is evidence of the persistence of ethnic practice in the Delta. It is full of Chinese produce: long bean, fuzzy melon, bitter melon, winter melon, Chinese eggplant, Chinese okra, Chinese cress, and joujou.

The garden is built in the ruins of a farm camp that once housed so many workers it had a three-wok kitchen. Now the bunkhouses are falling down; the bathhouse is boarded up; the water tower is empty; and the whole place has become an excuse for an elaborate, beautiful series of trellises.

Just beyond the edges of the Delta, the pattern of land subdivision that comes from the rivers is replaced by the relentless logic of the survey grid.

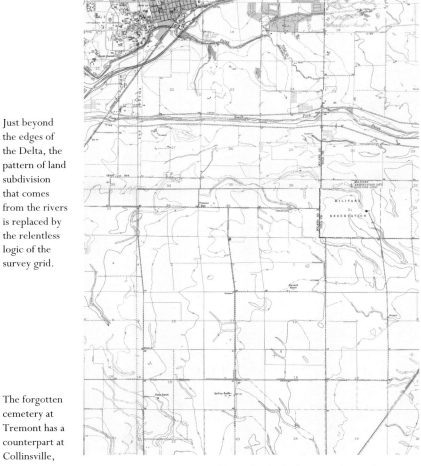

The forgotten cemetery at Tremont has a counterpart at Collinsville, in the Montezuma Hills. Located at the margins of the Delta, both places are also on the margins of our consciousness: rural life is more and more remote from our everyday experience, and death is more and more hidden from view.

Map 8   66

5 ✹

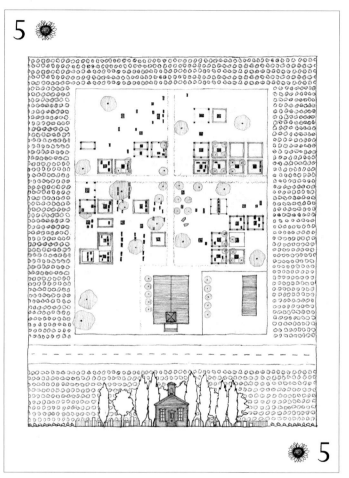

Situated among the fields and subdivided like a garden, the Tremont Cemetery turns an urban type—the churchyard burial ground—into an agrarian landscape.

What makes the graveyard different from surroundings, apart from its special use, is its trees. They are the only vertical relief in this very flat place, and the shade they create offers respite from the intense heat and bright light of the Yolo County sun.

✹ **5**

Memory Garden

When the
Delta was
remote, most
agricultural
workers lived
in farm camps.
Now many of
them live in
the towns and
cities at the
Delta's edges
and drive to
work.

Map 44   68

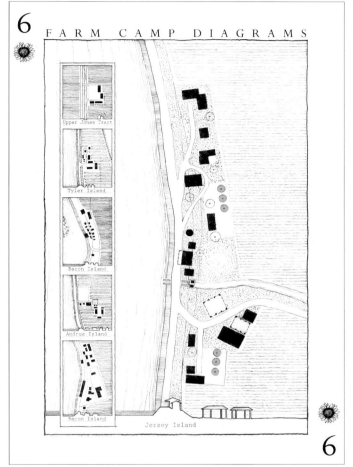

6 FARM CAMP DIAGRAMS

Upper Jones Tract

Tyler Island

Bacon Island

Andrus Island

Bacon Island

Jersey Island

The farm camps in the Delta are almost always located between the river and the fields. They act like tiny cities: they're dense, and they accommodate work life, domestic life, and social life. There are often packing sheds on the levees because produce used to be transported by boat.

6

The farm camps are full of small gardens. They are ramshackle but charming, like the hamlets in a picturesque landscape.

At first
Discovery Bay
was more like
a playground
than a suburb.
It was not
attached to a
city, and the
Delta was still
far away from
most places.
Since then,
Stockton,
Tracy, and the
Bay Area have
expanded, and
now Discovery
Bay is
inhabited by
commuters.

Map 39

70

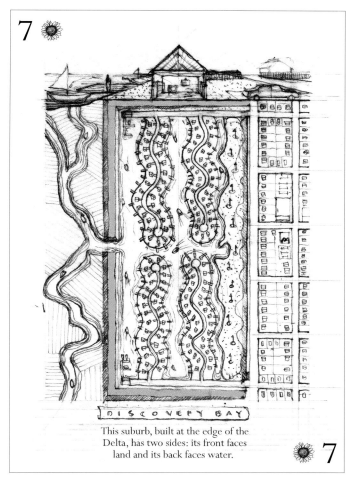

At Discovery Bay the house becomes a fulcrum between the route of the car and the route of the boat: drive in from the routine of the city, and sail out in search of adventure on the rivers of the Delta.

The suburban cul-de-sac has been reconfigured for ideal access to nature.

DISCOVERY BAY

This suburb, built at the edge of the Delta, has two sides: its front faces land and its back faces water.

Discovery Bay reframes the Delta. From its vantage point, the rivers are an extension of the backyard, and the islands exist to occupy the space between the watercourses.

The Cosumnes
is the only
undammed
river on the
western slope
of the Sierra
Nevada. The
Cosumnes
River Preserve
is the first
place in the
Delta where
levees have
been taken
away.

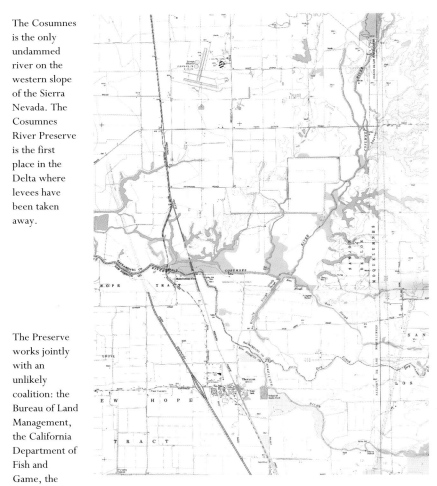

The Preserve
works jointly
with an
unlikely
coalition: the
Bureau of Land
Management,
the California
Department of
Fish and
Game, the
California Department of Water Resources, the Sacramento
County Department of Regional Parks, Ducks Unlimited, the
Nature Conservancy, and the Wildlife Conservation Board.

Map 23   72

8 🌻

Cultivation takes different forms at the Cosumnes River Preserve. Some of the land is used for sustainable agriculture, and the rest is devoted to raising wetlands.

At the Cosumnes River Nature Preserve the Nature Conservancy is transforming farm land at the river's edge to native wetland and grassland habitat and cultivating other land seasonally.

Managed to present an image of nature, the Preserve is for humans as much as plants and animals. People go there to take walks, or watch birds, or canoe, or plant native oak trees.

🌻 **8**

The levees in the lower Delta are built to equal standards so that everyone is at the same risk for flooding. Making the levee around one island substantially stronger would endanger the neighbors.

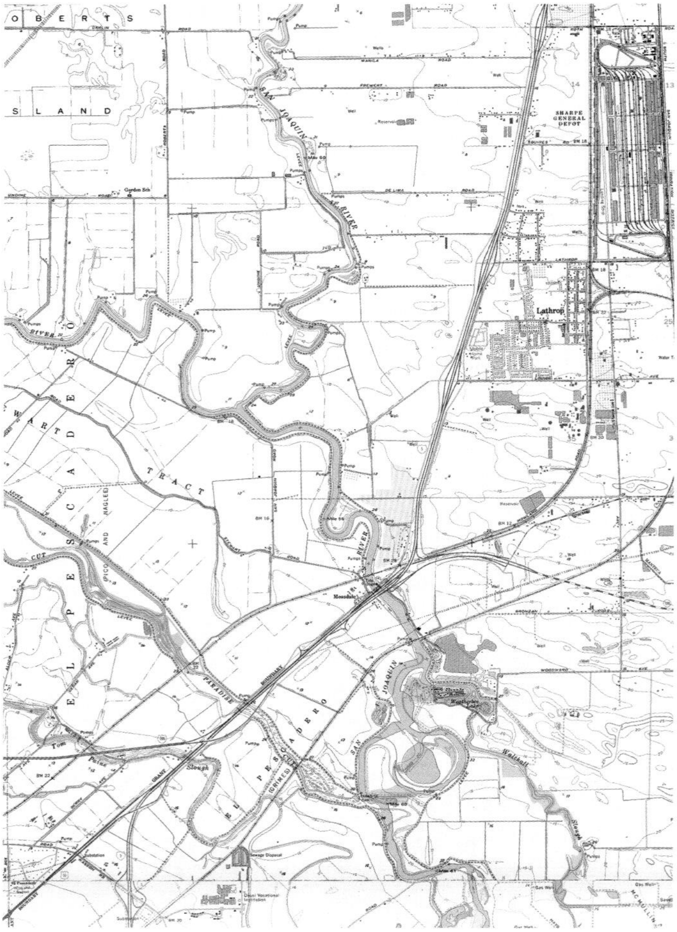

Stewart Tract is at the corner of a triangle between Stockton, Sacramento, and San Francisco. It would have been part of the Primary Zone of the Delta, where major development is prohibited, but a project had already been approved for the land. It is one of the last possible sites for urbanization in the Delta.

Map 48   74

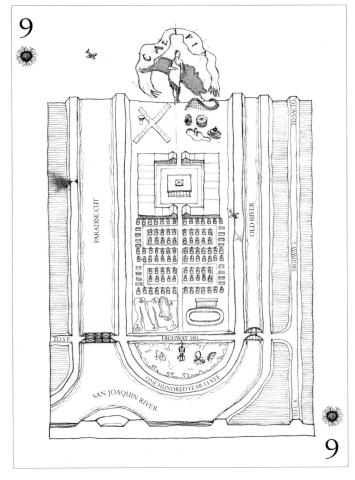

The first Califia was a mythical queen for whom California was named.

The new Califia was known first as Gold Rush City; now it has been renamed River Islands. The program has stayed the same: shopping centers, amusement parks, a stadium, an airfield, a golf course, wetlands, and 12,000 units of housing.

Stories about Paradise say that the garden is the creation of an entire world in miniature. The perfect world proposed for Stewart Tract exactly matches the vision of late 20th-century capitalism.

In the dry
season (and in
dry years),
the land in the
Yolo Bypass is
cultivated.
When the
Sacramento
River floods, it
is a spillway.
The crops in
the bypass are
restricted:
they may not
impede the
flow of
floodwaters.

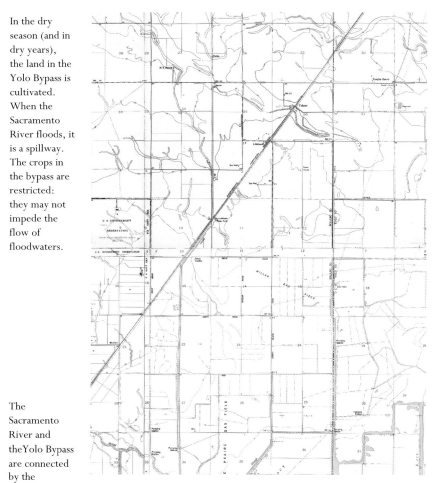

The
Sacramento
River and
theYolo Bypass
are connected
by the
Sacramento Weir. When the water level at the I Street gage in
Sacramento reaches 27.5 feet the Department of Water Resources begins
to open the 48 gates of the weir. The bypass is flooded to save the city.

Map 14   76

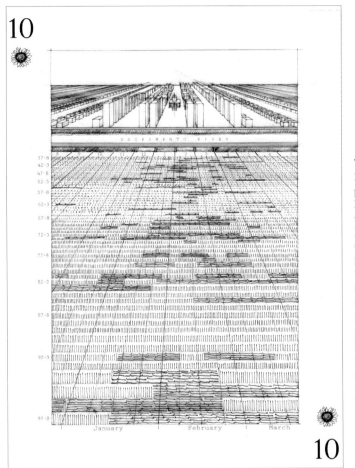

SACRAMENTO RIVER

37-8
42-3
47-8
52-3

57-8

62-3

67-8

72-3

77-8

82-3

87-8

92-3

97-8

January   February   March

The Yolo Bypass is productive land in more than one way. Most of the time it can be farmed. When flooding interferes with farming, the bypass provides habitat for wetland birds and it protects the city from high water.

The landscape is a negotiated solution to multiple needs.

Grant Line Road marks the boundary between two distinct patterns of land subdivision, one imposed by Spain and the other by the United States.

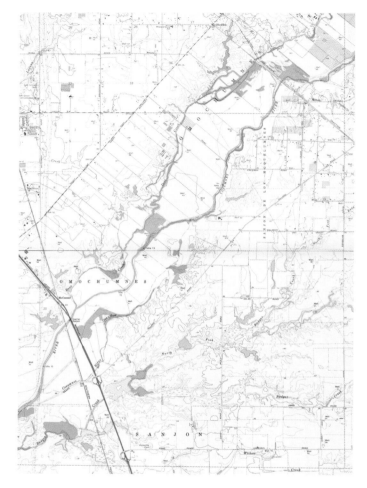

California was inhabited by the Spanish from 1679 to 1821 and by the Mexicans from 1821 to 1846. The land grants made by those regimes were honored when the state was subdivided according to the United States survey grid. Traces of Spanish culture remain in the law as well as in the landscape: old Spanish pueblo rights to water supersede claims based on later Anglo-American doctrines of appropriation, riparian right, and prescriptive right.

Map 18   78

j ✻

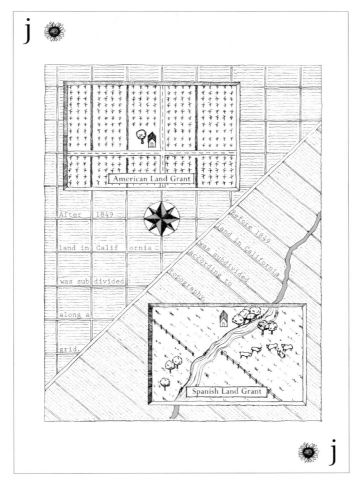

The American land grants assumed small holdings and water-intensive farming. Water rights were based on doctrines of private rights.

The Hispanic grants were big. Hispanic agriculture was adapted to dry climates, and the right to water was determined by public authority.

✻ j

Settlement patterns, like legal doctrines, are evidence of cultural ideas about how to tame and inhabit a wild place.

Sacramento is
sprawling.

From 1990 to
2000, the
population
of the
Sacramento
Principal
Metropolitan
Statistical Area
grew 21%. In
the ten years
before that, it
grew 35.8%.
The city is
growing at its
edges, not in
its center.

Like Stockton,
Lodi, Tracy,
and the cities of the Bay Area,
Sacramento is impinging on the Delta.

Map 10   80

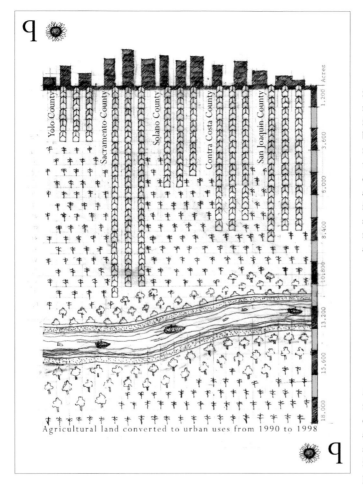

Agricultural land converted to urban uses from 1990 to 1998

Suburbs replace farmland because so many people want their own gardens: agricultural fields are subdivided to make quarter-acre lots.

As more and more land is developed, areas that are still open seem increasingly precious.

Expanding cities make an almost continuous perimeter around the Delta. Soon the landscape will seem like their collective garden, a backyard for the ring of development.

Mount Diablo is the most important landmark in the Delta: it can be seen from everywhere.

Because of its height and its immutability, the mountain served as the benchmark for the survey of California. In 1851, the year after the Swamp and Overflowed Lands Act made the Delta available for reclamation, the initial point of the survey was staked at the summit. From there the Mount Diablo Meridian and Baseline were extended and standard meridians and parallels were drawn at 24-mile intervals. That grid was divided into townships and sections, and the land in California was claimed. Now the Delta is much lower than it was in 1851, but the Initial Point is still the same.

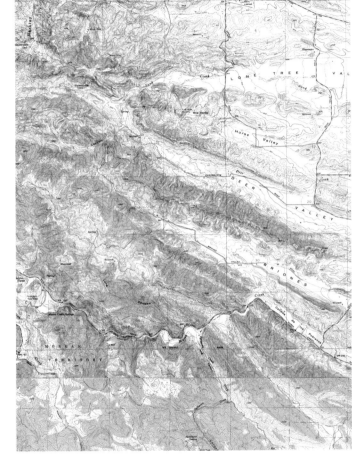

Map 37   82

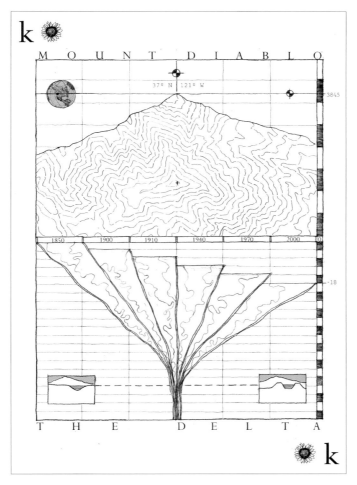

Mount Diablo is a constant presence in the flat landscape of the Delta: it is always visible, even in the bowls of the islands. The mountain is a landmark. Its place on the horizon tells you where you are.

Being able to fix your place and find your way is the first step in the domestication of the landscape.

Mount Diablo looms over the Delta like Mount Fuji in a Japanese painting: the mountain is the sublime presence in the garden.

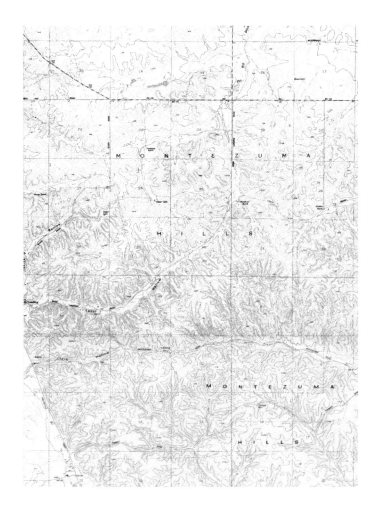

Map 25   84

Machine is the set of artifacts and practices people develop to exploit and control the natural forces in the landscape. Some machines are physical structures; others are management strategies; others are legal, political, and economic mechanisms.

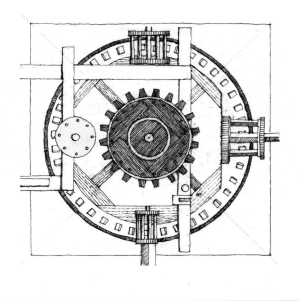

The aqueducts and the highway were built to convey valuable material—water and goods—from one place to another.

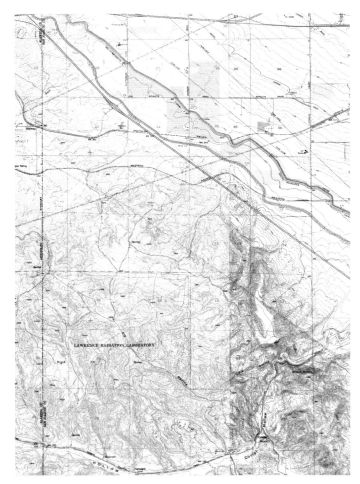

The story of Togo Shima and the headquarters building prefigures the aqueducts and the highway. It casts the river as a tool: a piece of transportation infrastructure.

Map 52   86

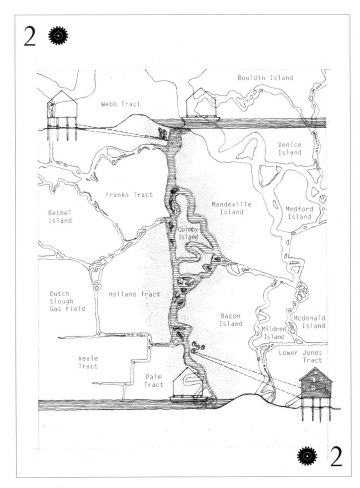

Togo Shima, sometimes known as the Potato King of the Delta, had two ranches, one on Webb Tract and one on Bacon Island. In the 1920s or so, he decided to move the headquarters of his outfit from Webb to Bacon.

The headquarters building had been built on stilts to protect it from floodwaters. He took the building off its stilts, put it on a barge, and floated it to Bacon Farm Camp Number 3, where it still stands.

After World War I, sugar beets became one of the Delta's main crops. There were two refineries in the Delta, one at Tracy and one at Clarksburg, and another nearby, at Manteca.

From the 1920s through the 1950s, about eight percent of the land under cultivation in the Delta was planted with sugar beets. The crop was grown most consistently in the mineral soils along the Sacramento River and in the Yolo Basin.

Map 3   88

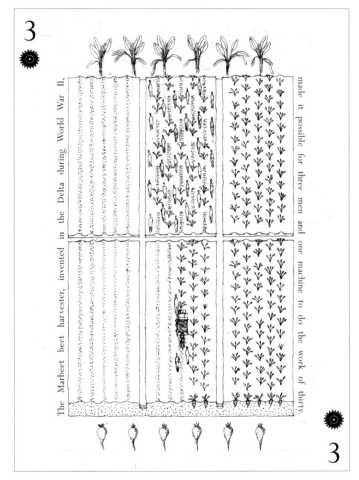

The Marbeet beet harvester, invented in the Delta during World War II, made it possible for three men and one machine to do the work of thirty.

Sugar beets were harvested by hand until the 1940s.

The labor shortage created by World War II inspired Lloyd Schmitt, a Rio Vista welder, to develop a beet harvester. The machine pulled beets from the ground and separated the leaves from the roots. Made by the Blackwelder Company of Rio Vista, it went into use all over the United States.

Mr. Schmitt's harvester was the product of tinkering and practicality. His shop was in the middle of the beet fields, and his intimate knowledge of the situation helped him find a solution that had eluded engineers from the agriculture school at Davis. His modest invention, developed from materials he had at hand, transformed beet cultivation in the Delta and across the country.

The Dutra
Museum of
Dredging is in
an old house
on Saint
Gertrude's
Avenue in Rio
Vista. There is
a clamshell
bucket in the
front yard.

The Dutra
Dredging
Company,
which operates
sidedraft
clamshell
dredgers in the
Delta, is just
north of town.

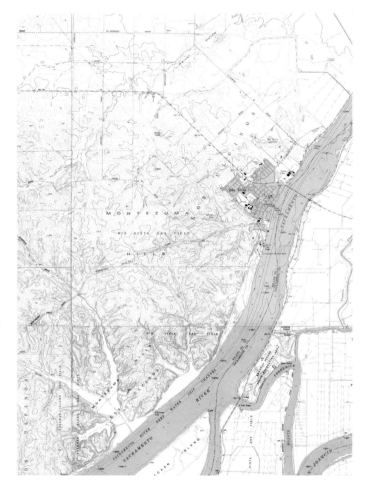

Map 26   90

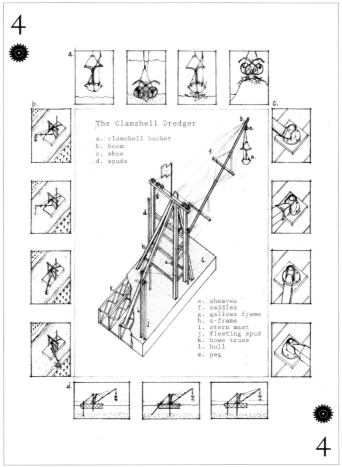

The Clamshell Dredger

a. clamshell bucket
b. boom
c. shoe
d. spuds

e. sheaves
f. saddles
g. gallows frame
h. a-frame
i. stern mast
j. fleeting spud
k. howe truss
l. hull
m. peg

Dredging technology made the large-scale reclamation of the Delta feasible. The sidedraft clamshell dredger was first used in the region in 1879. It won out over competing machines: the dipper dredge, the hydraulic pipeline dredge, and the bucket-ladder dredge.

Clamshell dredgers are still used for routine maintenance in the Delta. They do emergency service when a levee breach occurs.

Before the
Delta
was reclaimed,
the rivers
meandered
and the
perimeters of
the islands
were large
compared to
their areas.

The region's
early farmers
wanted
reclamation to
be profitable.
They cut off
the loops in
the rivers'
courses to
minimize the
length (and
cost) of the
levees relative
to the area of
land that could
be cultivated.

Efficiency of
construction
created two kinds of landscape: the large agricultural
islands and the small channel islands that were left over.

Map 40   92

5 ☀

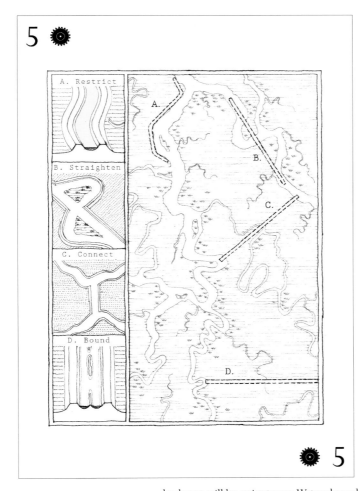

Restricting means confining the course of the river with levees. Straightening creates a shortcut across the river's meandering path. Connecting makes links between rivers that do not cross. Bounding uses drainage channels to mark property lines.

☀ **5**

All of these interventions are made so that the landscape will be easier to use. Water channels can't move; their banks don't overflow; distances are shorter; navigation is simpler; ownership is clear. The flux of the rivers is arrested, at least for the moment.

The Stockton
Deep Water
Channel, dug
in the 1930s,
makes it
possible for
ocean-going
vessels to
reach the Port
of Stockton,
ninety miles
east of the
Golden Gate.

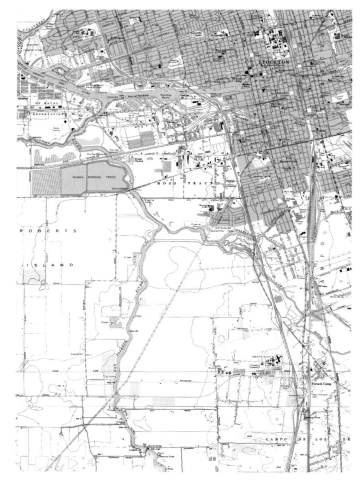

The port,
sited at the
east edge of
the Delta,
is the infrastructural joint between the Great Valley and the Pacific Ocean. Stockton has always
been an entrepot point: the city is a nexus where east-west routes meet north-south routes.

Map 42   94

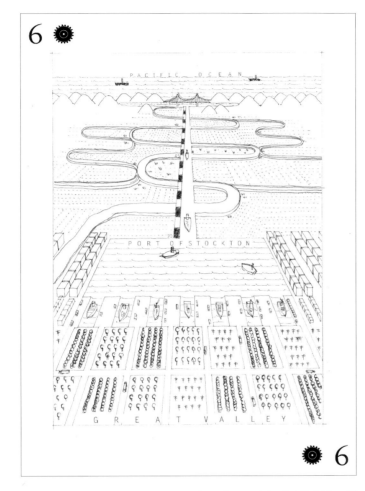

Ships come from as far away as China to pick up grain and other agricultural produce from the Valley.

The Stockton Deep Water Channel slices through the rivers and sloughs of the Delta: small pleasure boats sometimes find themselves next to giant freighters. The engine of the market has rationalized the transportation of produce: crops come into the port in trucks, and they go out in the same ships that will carry them around the world.

The Joint Operations Control Office is located in Sacramento, between the dams to the north and the water users to the south. Its activities control the flow of water through the Delta.

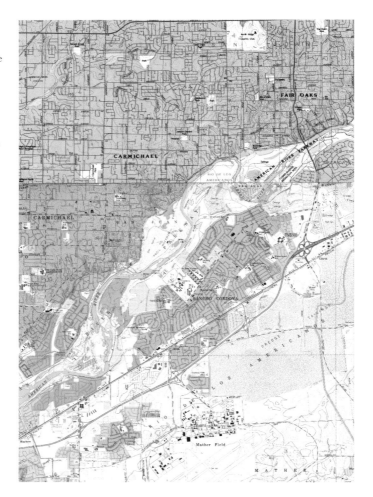

Map 6   96

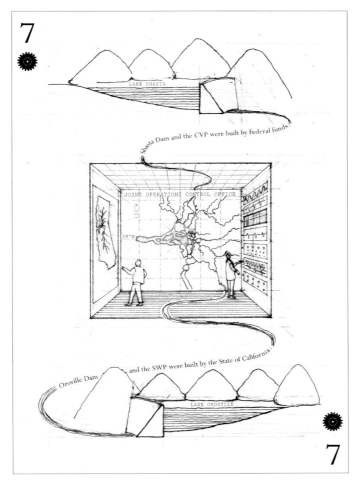

7

Shasta Dam and the CVP were built by Federal funds.

JOINT OPERATIONS CONTROL OFFICE

122°W

38°N

Oroville Dam and the SWP were built by the State of California.

LAKE SHASTA

LAKE OROVILLE

7

Shasta and Oroville Dams make the aqueducts possible: they provide a consistent water supply year round.

The Joint Operations Control Office calculates the demand for Central Valley Project and State Water Project water, makes releases from the dams, and regulates the pumps.

The enormous faucets of Shasta and Oroville Dams are opened and closed in Sacramento so that water can come out of the taps in the southern half of California.

In a water transfer, one entity, like the Kern County Water Agency, sells the water to which it has rights to another entity, like the San Diego County Water Authority. Water transfers are independent of geography: the only requirement besides buyers and sellers is the means to transport the water to its destination.

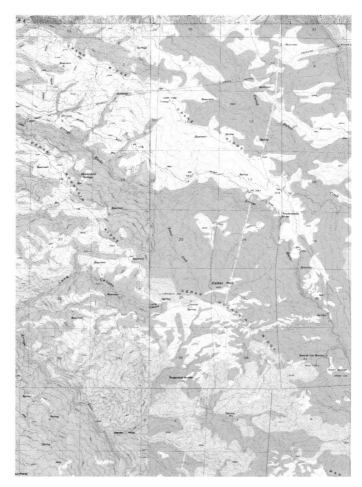

Map 57   98

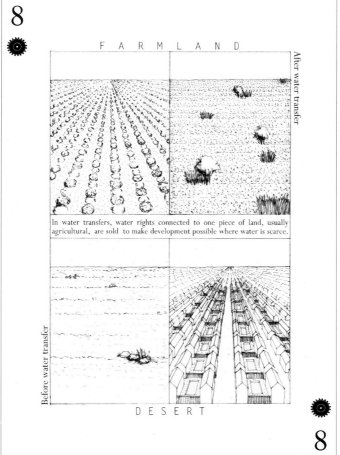

8

FARMLAND

After water transfer

In water transfers, water rights connected to one piece of land, usually agricultural, are sold to make development possible where water is scarce.

Before water transfer

DESERT

8

Transfers involve the redistribution of water, not the production of more supplies. The water doesn't actually travel from buyer to seller: Kern County just takes less out of the aqueduct, and San Diego takes more.

Water has become a valuable commodity. Provided to farmers at subsidized rates, it is sold to cities for its market value.

The State of
California is
obliged to
maintain fresh
water in the
river channels
for farmers:
if the water
that moves
through the
soil turns salty,
land is hard to
cultivate.
After salt
water
migrated
upstream, the
State agreed to
buy Sherman
Island and
Twitchell
Island from
their owners.
Salts had
leached into
the soil, and
the land could
no longer be
farmed at a
profit.

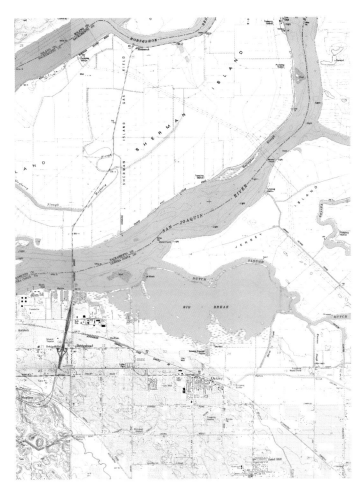

Map 32   100

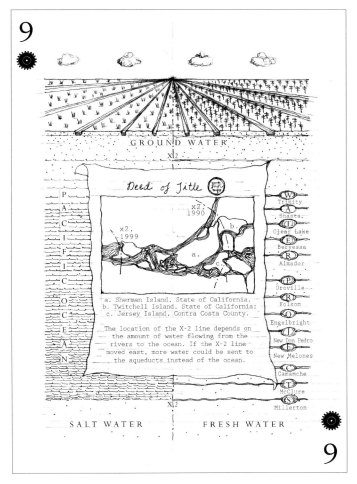

9

GROUND WATER

x2

Deed of Title

x2
1990

x2
1999

b.

a.

c.

a. Sherman Island. State of California.
b. Twitchell Island. State of California;
c. Jersey Island. Contra Costa County.

The location of the X-2 line depends on
the amount of water flowing from the
rivers to the ocean. If the X-2 line
moved east, more water could be sent to
the aqueducts instead of the ocean.

P A C I F I C   O C E A N

W A T E R
Trinity
Shasta.
Clear Lake
Beryessa
Almador
Oroville
Folsom
Engelbright
New Don Pedro
New Melones
Camanche
McClure
Millerton

x2

SALT WATER   FRESH WATER

9

The quality of the groundwater moving through the Delta depends on its relation to the X-2 line, where salty water from the bay meets fresh water from the rivers. The location of the X-2 line depends on the amount of water released from dams upstream and on the amount of water diverted from the rivers to the aqueducts. By buying land at the mouth of the Delta, the state absolves itself of the responsibility to maintain fresh water for the owners of farm land. Less water needs to flow west; more can be sent south. Land ownership has become a tool for the allocation of water.

Clifton Court Forebay used to be land. Its purpose is to allow sediment to drop out of the water that goes to the aqueducts. There are two sets of pumps at the forebay, one for the State Water Project and one for the Central Valley Project.

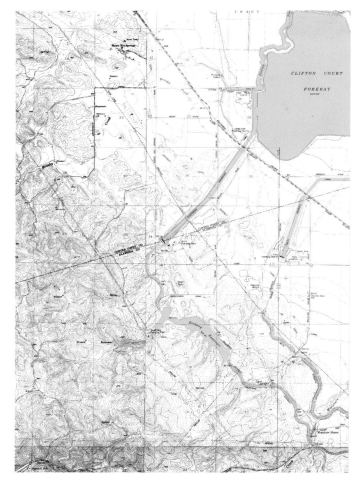

There is also a Fish Protective Facility, where fish are taken out of the water before it is pumped over the hills. The facility was built because large-scale pumping changed the currents in the Delta and confused anadromous fish: they swam toward the pumps instead of toward the ocean.

Map 45 102

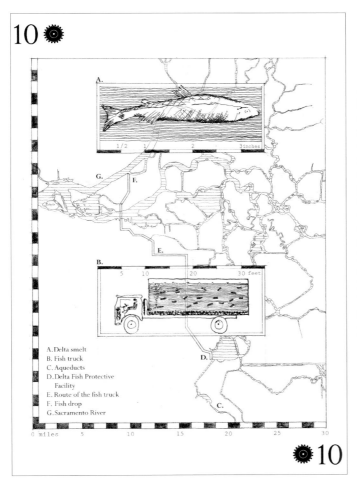

10 ✺

A.

G. F.

E.

B.

A. Delta smelt
B. Fish truck
C. Aqueducts
D. Delta Fish Protective
  Facility
E. Route of the fish truck
F. Fish drop
G. Sacramento River

D.

C.

0 miles   5   10   15   20   25   30

✺**10**

At the FPF, fish are screened from the water, weighed, measured, recorded, and put into a tanker truck that drives them to the Sacramento River, near the mouth of the Delta and beyond the reach of the pumps.

The fish truck is part infrastructure, part performance art: the route of the fish has been reinvented so that water can be sent to the Central Valley and Southern California. Behind this ritual lies a legislative machine: the process is undertaken on behalf of threatened and endangered species protected by the Environmental Protection Act and the California Environmental Quality Act.

Two aqueducts carry water from the Delta to the south. The Delta-Mendota was built by the Federal government to supply farmers in the Central Valley with irrigation water. The California Aqueduct was built by the State of California to provide water to Los Angeles.

There are no fixed limits on the export of water from the Delta. The current mandates are to pump as

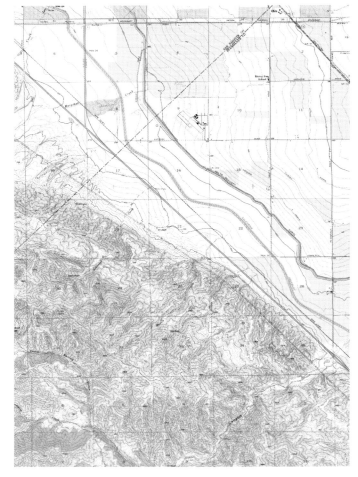

much water as possible out of the rivers and to maintain the quality of the environment. One of the central questions in the water politics of the Delta is what constitutes acceptable environmental health: the range of the acceptable is defined differently by different constituents of the landscape.

Map 60   104

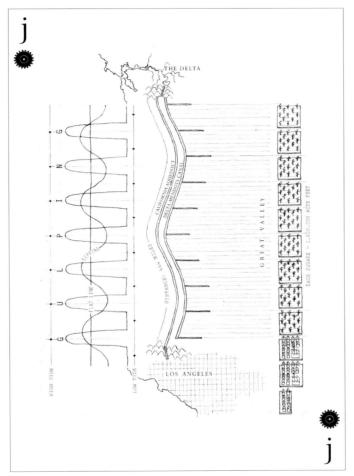

There are different protocols for pumping water out of the Delta. Ecologists and local farmers advocate gulping because it minimizes effects on water levels in the rivers. People on the delivery end prefer flatline pumping because it delivers a constant supply.

Sacramento is the capital of California, and the state agencies that manage the Delta have their headquarters there.

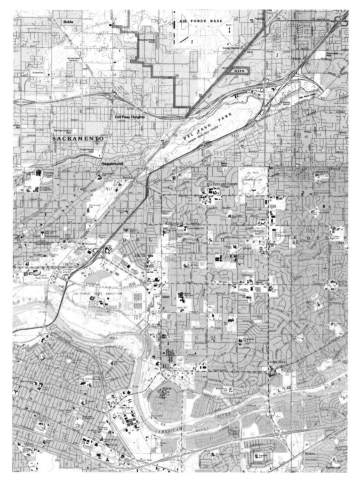

The city looks like a cross between Washington, D. C. and any of the farm towns in the Great Central Valley. California's population growth has meant more and more state government, and that has made Sacramento a boom town.

Map 5　　　106

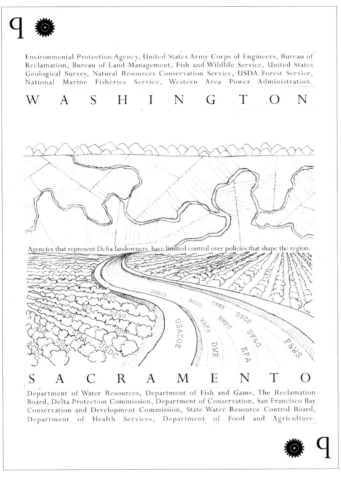

q ⚙

Environmental Protection Agency, United States Army Corps of Engineers, Bureau of Reclamation, Bureau of Land Management, Fish and Wildlife Service, United States Geological Survey, Natural Resources Conservation Service, USDA Forest Service, National Marine Fisheries Service, Western Area Power Administration.

W A S H I N G T O N

Agencies that represent Delta landowners have limited control over policies that shape the region.

S A C R A M E N T O

Department of Water Resources, Department of Fish and Game, The Reclamation Board, Delta Protection Commission, Department of Conservation, San Francisco Bay Conservation and Development Commission, State Water Resource Control Board, Department of Health Services, Department of Food and Agriculture.

⚙ q

The Delta falls under the jurisdiction of many different regulatory agencies.

The future is being determined in large part by distant powers: Washington and Sacramento.

The agencies that manage the Delta represent the view that the landscape can be controlled.

The government organizes and manages the landscape as a series of functional categories like agriculture, wildlife conservation, or flood prevention.

The suburbs of Sacramento, like those of Stockton, Tracy, and the Bay Area, are encroaching on the Delta. Rapid population growth has made the city into a metropolis.

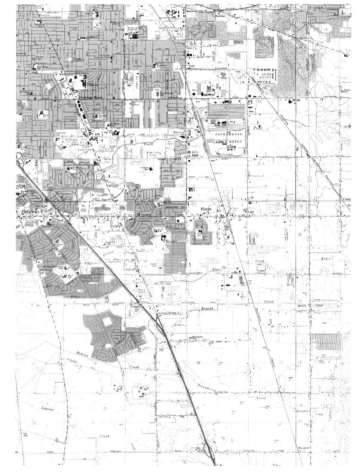

This map of suburban Sacramento can be read as the sum of individual actions: it represents an expanding number of acres filled, house by house, with hoses, toilets, showers, sinks, dishwashers, washing machines, and leaky pipes.

Map 11   108

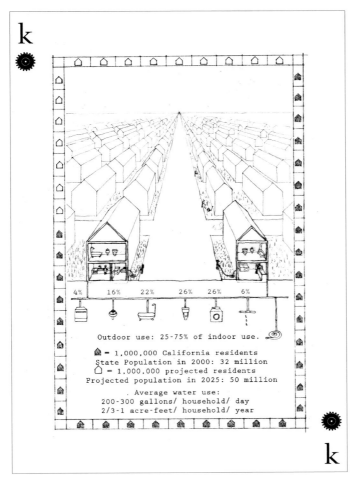

k

4%   16%   22%   26%   26%   6%

Outdoor use: 25-75% of indoor use.

⌂ = 1,000,000 California residents
State Population in 2000: 32 million
⌂ = 1,000,000 projected residents
Projected population in 2025: 50 million

. Average water use:
200-300 gallons/ household/ day
2/3-1 acre-feet/ household/ year

Suburban houses are filled with machines and devices that use water. The urge to buy more and more appliances is an expression of the engine of consumption at a domestic, individual scale.

Each house is another end of the line for the urban water delivery system.

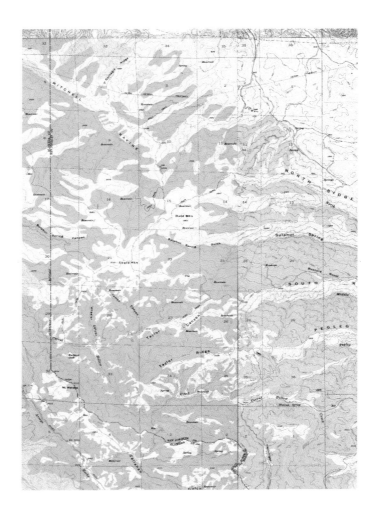

Map 58

110

Wilderness is the set of processes and phenomena that people don't (and can't) control. Sometimes wilderness is suddenly and directly visible. In other cases it transforms the landscape incrementally, and we can only read its work over time and by inference.

The Peripheral Canal and Highway 5 were meant as twins: one was to move people across the state, and the the other was to move water. The canal would have taken water from the Sacramento River at Hood and carried it around the edge of the Delta, straight to the aqueducts. It was defeated in a 1982 referendum by voters who feared it would starve the Delta of water.

Map 29   112

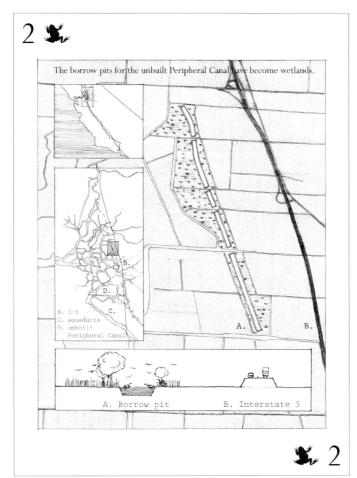

The borrow pits for the unbuilt Peripheral Canal have become wetlands.

B. I-5
C. aqueducts
D. unbuilt
Peripheral Canal

A. Borrow pit   B. Interstate 5

B.

A.   B.

The borrow pits that follow Highway 5 along the edge of the Delta were supposed to have been part of the Peripheral Canal. The canal was never finished, though, and the abandoned trenches became habitat for wetland plants and animals.

Conceived as a machine, the borrow pits have become a wilderness.

🐸 2

The hills of the Diablo and Coast Ranges separate the Delta and the Great Valley from the ocean.

Map 43

114

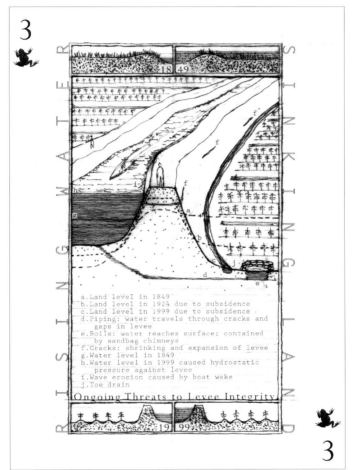

3

RISING WATER SINKING LAND

a. Land level in 1849
b. Land level in 1924 due to subsidence
c. Land level in 1999 due to subsidence
d. Piping: water travels through cracks and gaps in levee
e. Boils: water reaches surface: contained by sandbag chimneys
f. Cracks: shrinking and expansion of levee
g. Water level in 1849
h. Water level in 1999 caused hydrostatic pressure against levee
i. Wave erosion caused by boat wake
j. Toe drain

Ongoing Threats to Levee Integrity

3

The levees built when the Delta was reclaimed made high river levels higher by limiting the flood plain. They made ordinary levels higher, too, because alluvial sediment that was once carried onto the flood plain was now deposited in the river channels, and the bottoms of the channels rose.

The levees were an attempt to create stasis in the landscape: their purpose was to stop seasonal flooding. Instead they just redirected the flux of the river system. Their effects, combined with subsidence, have created a dilemma that cannot be resolved.

Just above the Delta the San Joaquin River runs across land that is almost flat. The flatness of the terrain means that the water moves very slowly, and the river has developed a convoluted, meandering course.

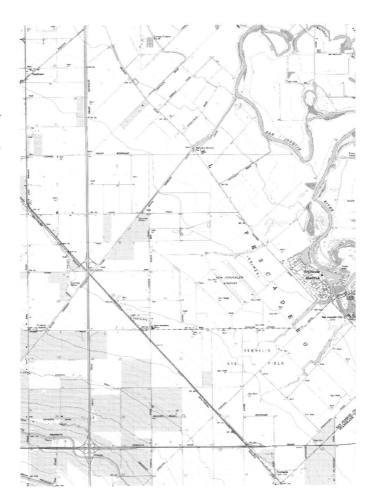

Map 54   116

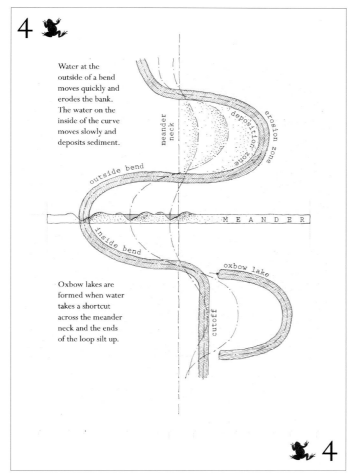

4 🐸

Water at the outside of a bend moves quickly and erodes the bank. The water on the inside of the curve moves slowly and deposits sediment.

meander neck

deposition zone

erosion zone

outside bend

MEANDER

inside bend

oxbow lake

cutoff

Oxbow lakes are formed when water takes a shortcut across the meander neck and the ends of the loop silt up.

🐸 4

The slower the movement of water in a river, the more winding its course.

The bends in a river become longer and closer together over time. At a certain point, water needs less energy to cut a new channel than to go around a meander, and the course straightens out again.

The rivers in the Delta meandered until they were fixed by the construction of the levees. Rivers that have not been constrained are constantly changing course: water always seeks the path of least resistance.

The Yolo Bypass, built to protect the city of Sacramento from flooding on the Sacramento River, can accommodate flows of 500,000 cubic feet of water per second; the river channel carries only 110,000 cubic feet per second.

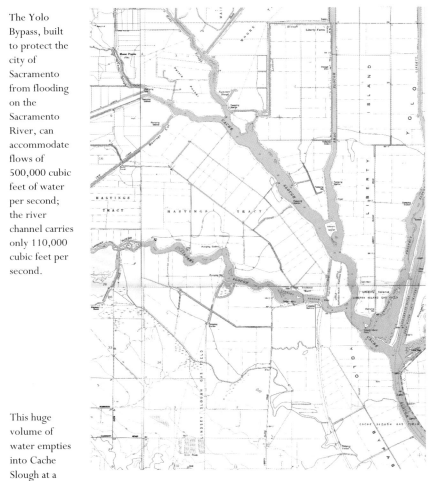

This huge volume of water empties into Cache Slough at a narrow point on the the southern end of the bypass. Originally designed as a row of culverts, the outlet was not always able to handle the water that backed up behind it.

Map 20   118

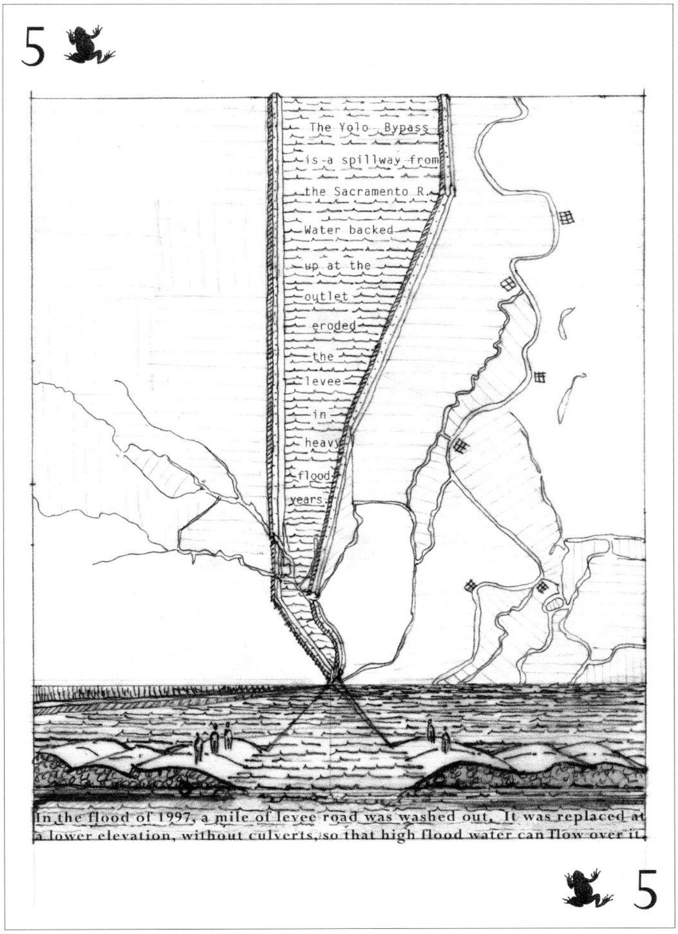
5
The Yolo Bypass
is a spillway from
the Sacramento R.
Water backed
up at the
outlet
eroded
the
levee
in
heavy
flood
years.
In the flood of 1997, a mile of levee road was washed out. It was replaced at
a lower elevation, without culverts, so that high flood water can flow over it.
5

In 1997 the Cache Slough levee buckled and crumpled under the force of the water at the bottleneck. What the flood left behind looked like earthquake damage.

The bypass circumvents the problem of flooding in Sacramento, but it does not diminish the violence of the water. Moving the flood is not the same as controlling it.

The channel
islands are a
byproduct of
reclamation.
Levee builders
cut off the
loops of rivers
to make
shortcuts and
to make the
islands' ratios
of area to edge
length as high
as possible.
The fragments
of leftover
land were too
small to
cultivate.

Map 34   120

6

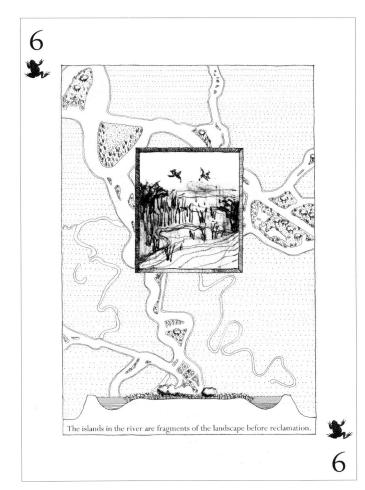

The islands in the river are fragments of the landscape before reclamation.

6

The islands in the river channels have been abandoned to nature. They flood, and they change. No one knows their exact areas or locations. Habitat for wetland plants and animals, they are occupied only tenuously by people, who must be prepared for their docks to wash away.

The channel islands are not far away from the cultivated land in the Delta, but they seem remote in time, like moments and places preserved from a long time ago.

Until World War II, most of the traffic in the Delta was on the rivers. Daily steamers carried passengers and freight from Sacramento to San Francisco, and smaller local boats delivered mail and ferried children to school.

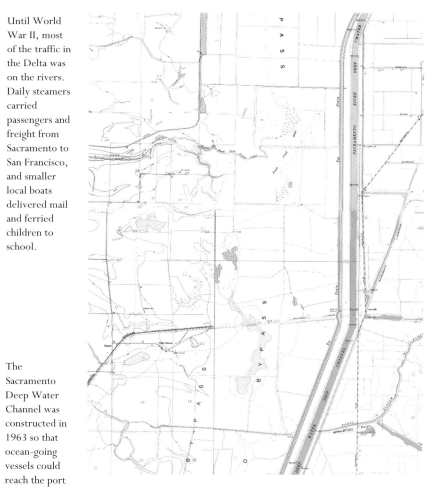

The Sacramento Deep Water Channel was constructed in 1963 so that ocean-going vessels could reach the port of Sacramento. Dug along a straight course miles away from the winding Sacramento River, it was designed like a highway: it was not as beautiful as the meandering rivers and sloughs that run through the Delta, but it eliminated the chance of getting lost.

Map 9   122

7

TULE FOG above the rivers meant that boats had to navigate by sounds reflected from an ECHO BOARD

7

Tule fog forms when water condenses in cool air just above the ground. It usually develops at night, and it covers the rivers and sloughs in a thick blanket.

The fog makes landmarks invisible: it even hides the banks of the river. It turns a familiar landscape into a mystery.

Franks Tract is a new landscape. It bears no resemblance to the marshes that existed before reclamation, and the island's agricultural past has been obliterated. Now the place is the province of boaters and windsurfers, and its neighbors are afraid of the erosive power of its waves.

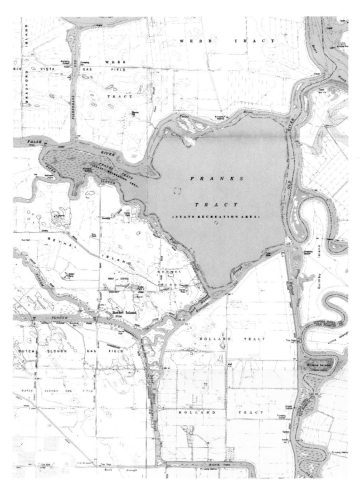

Map 33   124

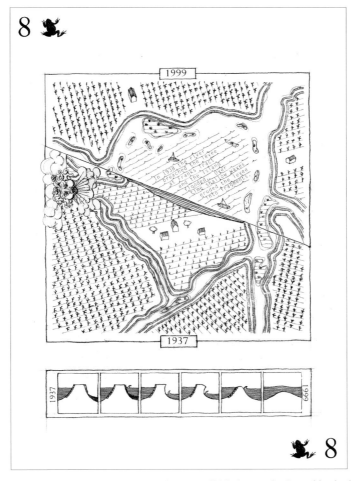

8 🐸

1999

In 1938 the river breached the levee at Franks Island and the tract flooded. Over time, shallow waves eroded the levee into fragments.

1937

The water that covered Franks Tract was shallow, but because of its width, the fetch created large, powerful waves. Over time they destroyed the levee almost completely.

The levee was undercut from the back side, where it was not reinforced.

🐸 8

The story of Franks Tract is about the compounding of uncontrollable forces. The farmed land subsided; there were heavy rains; the levee was breached; the wind created strong waves; the levee eroded beyond repair; and now the water threatens the neighbors. The landscape is a warning: if too many islands flood, the whole Delta will become a watery graveyard.

The California
Department of
Fish and Game
operated a
hatchery at Elk
Grove until
the early
1990s. The
hatchery,
located on
Laguna Creek,
raised warm-
water fish:
black bass and
striped bass.
It was closed
because those
species
reproduced
well enough
in lakes, on
their own.

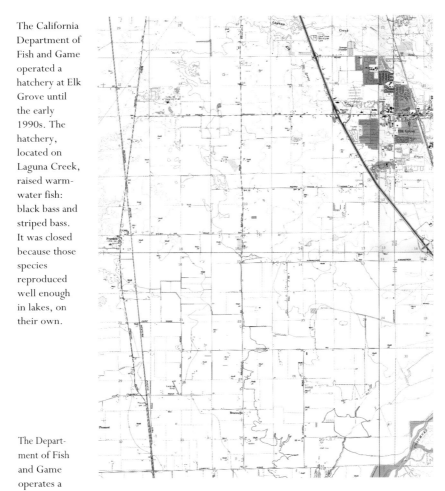

The Depart-
ment of Fish
and Game
operates a
number of hatcheries on rivers that drain into
the Delta. They raise steelhead and salmon on
the Mokolumne, American, and Feather Rivers.

Map 17   126

9

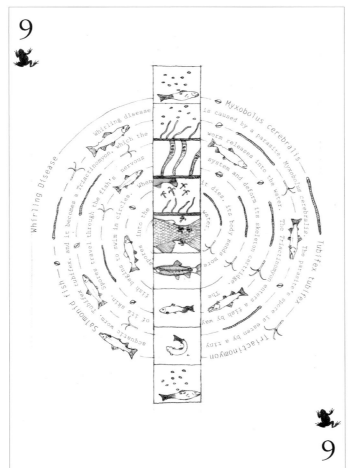

Whirling disease first appeared in California in 1965. It is found in several of the rivers that drain the Sierra Nevada, including the Mokolumne. It infects salmonid fish, mainly trout.

9

Even in situations that seem manageable, uncontrollable forces emerge. Hatcheries can become breeding grounds for epidemics as well as for fish.

The debris generated by hydraulic mining traveled through the rivers from the mountains to the Delta. It caused so much damage that court orders were issued to stop the process; they were the first significant environmental rules in the United States.

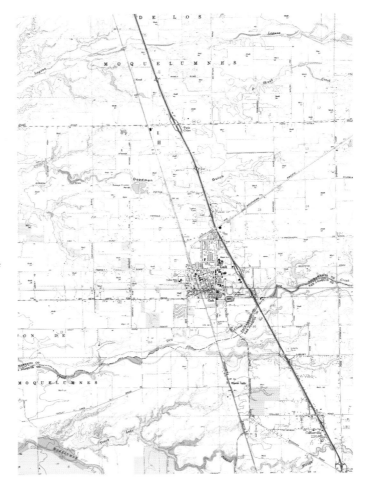

Map 24   128

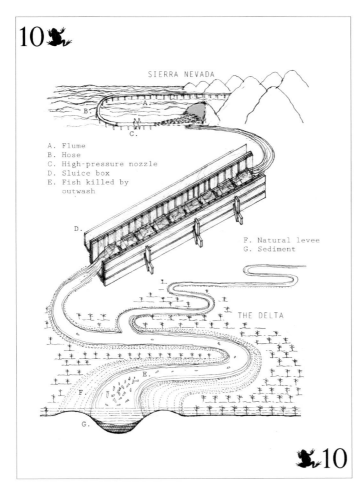

10

SIERRA NEVADA

A. Flume
B. Hose
C. High-pressure nozzle
D. Sluice box
E. Fish killed by
   outwash

F. Natural levee
G. Sediment

THE DELTA

10

Hydraulic gold mining used water to blast away the sides of mountains. The water went through a sluice box, where gold settled out and sediment washed through into the rivers.

The vast amounts of dirt that went into the rivers wrought havoc downstream in the Delta. The water turned brown with mud.

Fish choked and died from lack of oxygen. Stream channels filled with silt. Boat traffic became impossible. Flooding grew worse and worse. The landscape was devastated.

The mouth of
the Delta is at
the west end
of Sherman
Island, where
the San
Joaquin
and the
Sacramento
converge.
From there
they flow to
the bay and the
ocean.

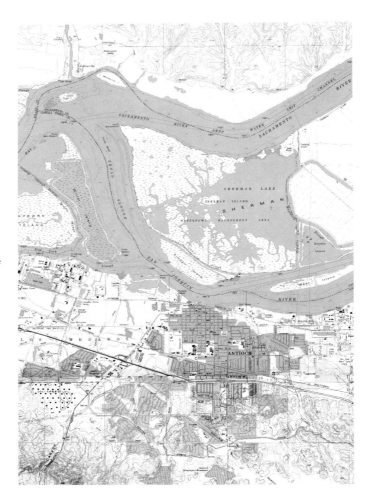

Map 31

130

native vs. exotic

The tule and cattail are native to California. They were among the most common plants in the Delta before reclamation. The Delta's peat soils come from the slow decomposition of these plants.

The water hyacinth is native to the Amazon delta. It was introduced to the United States at the Cotton States Exposition in New Orleans in 1884, and it was identified on the Sacramento River in 1904.

Tule, Cattail
Scirpus ssp., Typha ssp.

Water Hyacinth
Eichhornia crassipes

Tules and cattails root in soil. They live in shallow water, and they are able to survive tidal fluctuations in depth and salinity. River sediment collects around their roots and stems and makes new ground.

Water hyacinth can root in water as well as soil. It reproduces quickly, choking out all competitors, limiting the movement of water and light and exhausting the oxygen supply in the river. Its proliferation can cause flooding by displacing significant amounts of water.

There are dozens of invasive plant and animal species in the Delta. Some, like the striped bass, were introduced on purpose; others, like the water hyacinth, were accidents. They cannot be eradicated, and their unanticipated proliferation has changed the Delta's ecology permanently.

Sacramento is
a river town.
Located just
north of the
Delta, where
the American
meets the
Sacramento, it
has always
been subject to
the seasonal
changes in the
two rivers
and their
tributaries.

Map 4   132

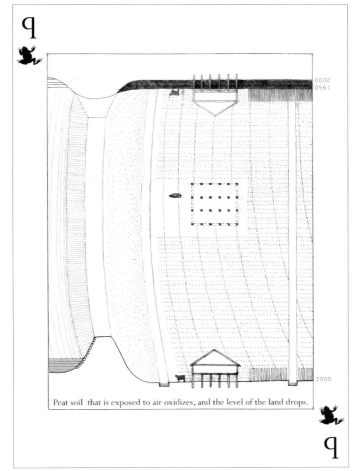

Peat soil that is exposed to air oxidizes, and the level of the land drops.

The land in the Delta has been subsiding since reclamation began. Surface elevations have fallen as low as 20 feet below sea level, and flooding is a constant threat.

Rivers and river landscapes change. Subsidence is evidence that efforts to control places like the Delta do not stop the fluctuation of natural processes: they merely cause it to take a different, unknown form. Cultivating land and building levees were supposed to make the landscape inhabitable and predictable. Instead, they made the ground disappear.

One farmer
manages all of
Staten Island.
After the
harvest, he
leaves the
stubble
standing in the
fields and
floods the
land.
Economies of
scale on the
farm mean that
some grain can
be left behind
as bird food.

Because the
operation is so
large, Staten
Island has
become an
important
stopping point
on the Pacific
Flyway.

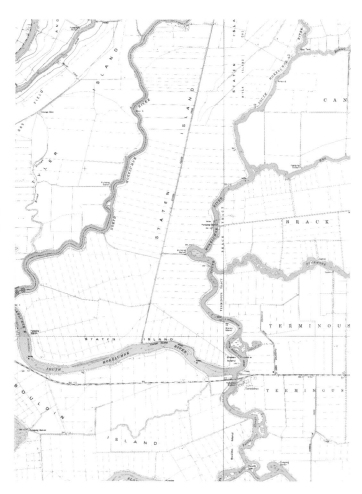

Map 28   134

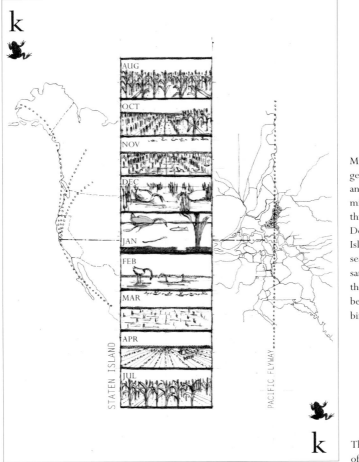

k

AUG

OCT

NOV

DEC

JAN

FEB

MAR

APR

JUL

STATEN ISLAND

PACIFIC FLYWAY

Millions of geese, swans, and ducks migrate through the Delta. Staten Island is a seasonal sanctuary. In the winter it belongs to the birds.

k

The flooding of the fields masks the difference between the river and the island. When that happens, the levee is the only visible souvenir of reclamation.

Map 51　　　　136

oy is the set of artifacts and practices contrived for pleasure and amusement and not for practical ends. Toys are meant to be played with. Sometimes they are objects; sometimes they are places; sometimes they are rituals; and sometimes they are metaphors.

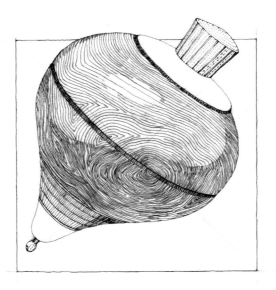

Ace of Toys

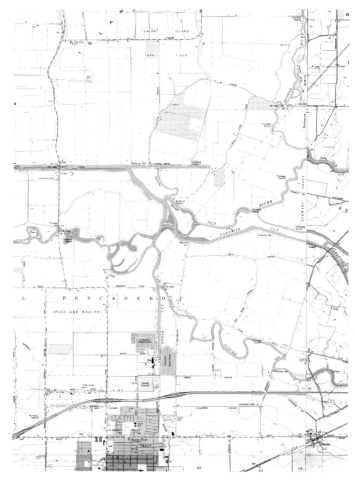

A tour of the figures in the map includes disappointments and pleasant surprises. Some of the places aren't as beautiful as the shapes they make on the map, but others, like the the intersection of the canal and the circle, are.

Map 47   138

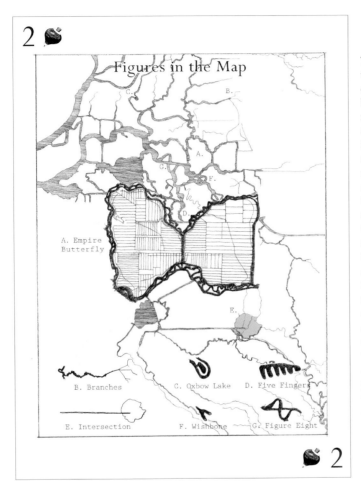

2 ✿

Figures in the Map

A. Empire
Butterfly

B. Branches   C. Oxbow Lake   D. Five Fingers

E. Intersection   F. Wishbone   G. Figure Eight

The figures in the map are conjunctions between natural form and human intervention: slips for boats are carved out of a small island, for instance, or the bends in a river are cut by a shipping channel. Finding them is inventing meaning in a series of accidental, uncoded shapes. The products of utility become raw material for daydreams.

✿ 2

The pears in the Delta follow the rivers: the orchards are planted just inside the levees on the alluvial soil of the old river banks. One of the strangest things about driving along the levee roads is seeing the tops of the trees below you.

Pears engender rituals. The Pear Fair is held every July in Courtland: people eat pear fritters, and the new Pear Queen is crowned.

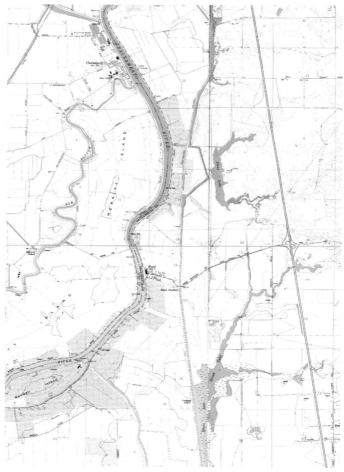

There are pear dynasties. The history of the north Delta can be told through the stories of old pear families like the McCormacks, the Wilsons, the Learys, the Eliots, the Greenes, the Caseys, the Mealers, the Van Lobensels, the Fongs, and the Gardeners.

Map 16   140

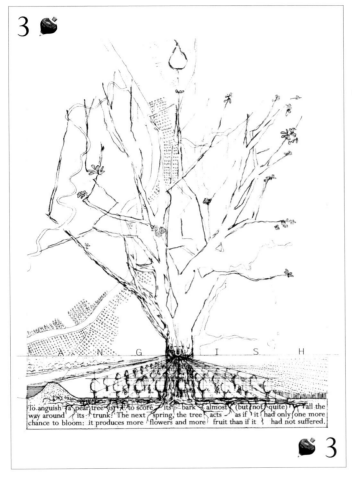

3

"Shade trees don't make fruit."

When asked why he raises different kinds of pears, Malcolm McCormack, a grower in the north Delta, said, "To play."

To anguish a pear tree is to score its bark almost (but not quite) all the way around its trunk. The next spring, the tree acts as if it had only one more chance to bloom: it produces more flowers and more fruit than if it had not suffered.

3

What is the relationship between a farmer and the plants he cultivates? Does a pear tree have a soul? What does the metaphor of anguishing describe? Is it the tree that suffers, or the farmer?

Houseboaters have autonomy: they do not need to spend the night on land. Their independence strengthens the sense that in the Delta, land and water are separate worlds.

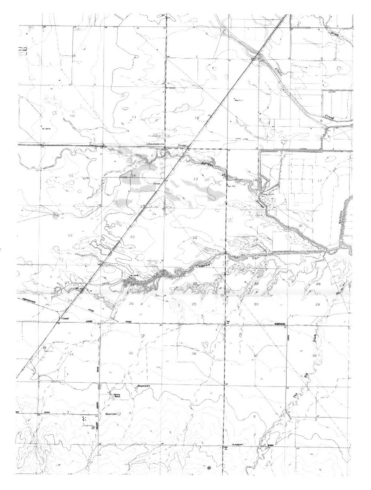

Map 19   142

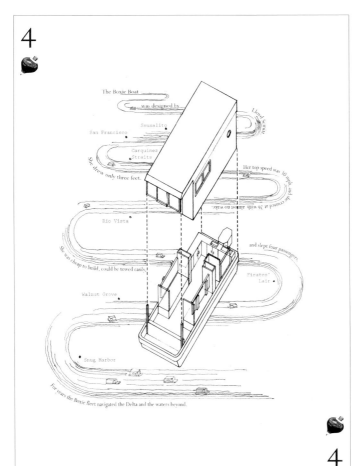

The Boxie Boat
was designed by
Lloyd Smith
Sausalito
San Francisco
Carquinez
Straits
She drew only three feet.
Her top speed was 30 mph, and she cruised at 26 with almost no wake.
Rio Vista
and slept four passengers.
She was cheap to build, could be towed easily,
Pirates' Lair
Walnut Grove
Snug Harbor
For years the Boxie fleet navigated the Delta and the waters beyond.

Made of off-the-shelf parts and easy to pilot, the Boxie Boat was a houseboat for Everyman.

A wide range of people bought Boxie Boats. They formed a Boxie Club, and they cruised together around the Delta and out to the Bay.

4

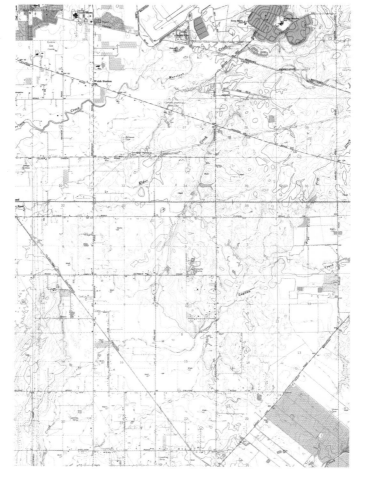

The Delta and
the farmland
that surrounds
it are thinly
settled.
The regular
gathering of
small groups of
people makes
a kind of
urbanity in the
quiet
countryside.

Map 12   144

The Happy Reading Club, founded in 1975, included ten members. They subscribed together to the *Chinese Times*, and they met in a former gambling house in Locke to read the paper and to eat.

Reading, which is often a solitary pursuit, became something to do with others for the pleasure of their company.

Most of the 17 ferries that operated in the Delta in 1958 have been replaced by bridges.

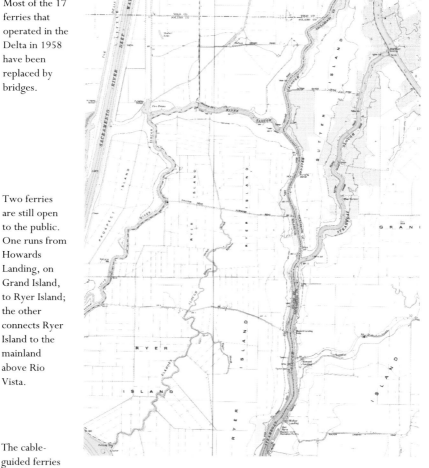

Two ferries are still open to the public. One runs from Howards Landing, on Grand Island, to Ryer Island; the other connects Ryer Island to the mainland above Rio Vista.

The cable-guided ferries are operated by the California Department of Transportation. Except for lunch and dinner breaks, they make crossings whenever passengers appear on the shore.

Map 21   146

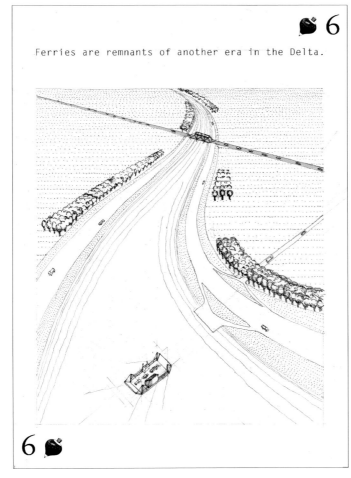

Ferries are remnants of another era in the Delta.

6

6

Ferries used to be part of everday life in the Delta.

In the 1950s, when Kyser Shimasaki was growing up on Bacon Island, the ferry stopped at 10:00. He and his friends paid the pilot $5 to run late on Saturday night.

Now the ferries are an adventure. It's a nostalgic pleasure to summon the pilot by waving from the opposite bank. The five-minute ride makes a direct connection between the world on land and the world on the river.

The Delta is a
sparsely settled
place. There
are a few
towns, but
most people
live in small
farm camps.
Located along
the rivers, the
camps are
more closely
connected by
water than by
land.

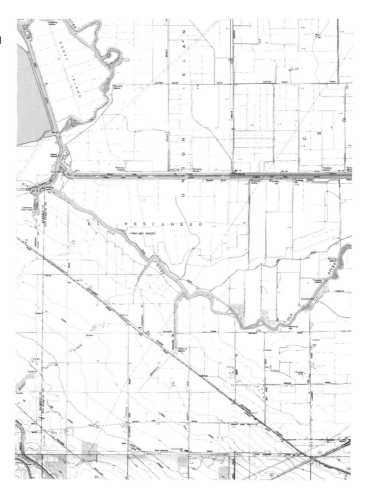

Map 46   148

7

COMING TO THE CANTINA FROM THE RIVERS AND THE FIELDS

7

Because the Delta is so empty, the camps have meaning at multiple scales. For many years the cantina at Bacon Island was a lunchroom for the camp's workers during the day, and at night it was a meeting place for people from the islands all around.

The cantina had two lives: during the day it was for working, but at night it was for playing.

The levees
were built in
large part by
Chinese
people who
had come to
California to
work on the
railroads.
Many of them
stayed in the
Delta and
became
agricultural
laborers.

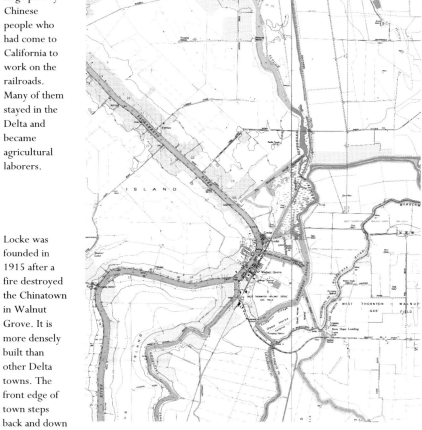

Locke was
founded in
1915 after a
fire destroyed
the Chinatown
in Walnut
Grove. It is
more densely
built than
other Delta
towns. The
front edge of
town steps
back and down
from the river: buildings that appear from the levee to be
one story high have two floors on the side that faces Main
Street. The back edge is a garden.

Map 22   150

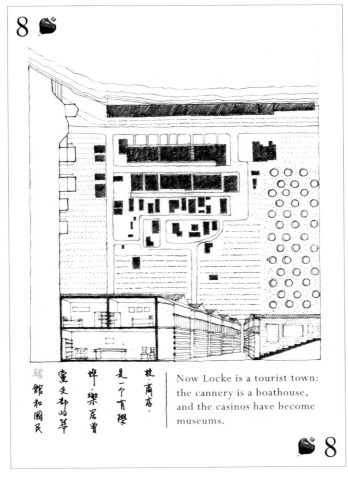

8

Locke was once busy: in the 1920s it had a flour mill, a movie theater, a post office, a school, a hotel, groceries, restaurants, speakeasies, brothels, opium dens, gambling houses, Chinese secret societies, and a branch of the Kuomintang.

Now Locke is a tourist town: the cannery is a boathouse, and the casinos have become museums.

賭館和國民
堂文部的等
埠·樂居費
是一个有樂
枝商店·

8

The exoticism of vice has been replaced by the exoticism of decay. The town is nearly deserted except for stray cats and tourists, who come to look at the remains of America's only rural Chinatown.

Stockton is the
county seat of
San Joaquin
County.

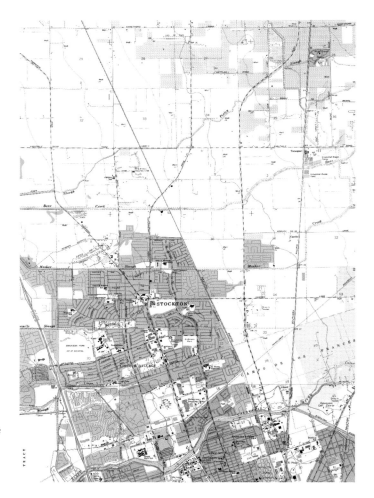

Map 36   152

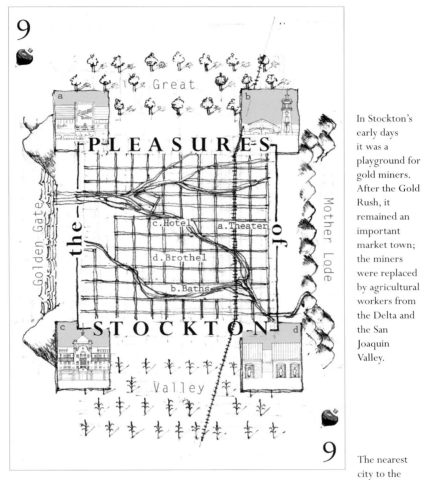

PLEASURES

the   of

STOCKTON

Golden Gate

Mother Lode

Great

Valley

c.Hotel   a.Theater

d.Brothel

b.Baths

In Stockton's
early days
it was a
playground for
gold miners.
After the Gold
Rush, it
remained an
important
market town;
the miners
were replaced
by agricultural
workers from
the Delta and
the San
Joaquin
Valley.

The nearest
city to the
lower Delta, Stockton has always offered
a wide variety of amusements.

Duck Days festivities are centered in Davis, but field trips and other activities reach into the Sacramento Valley.

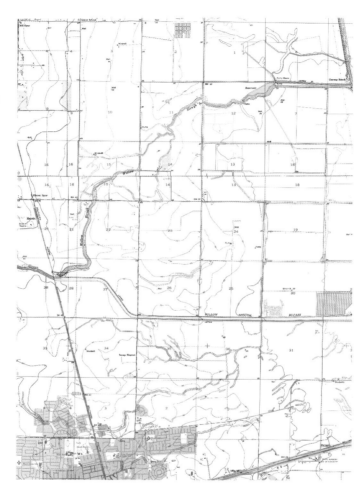

The festival's sponsors include groups whose points of view might not seem compatible: the City of Davis, the Sierra Club, the California Waterfowl Association, Capital Public Radio, and the U.S. Bureau of Reclamation were all significant financial contributors to the 2002 celebration.

Map 2   154

10

February 15, 16, 17 / near Davis

DUCK DAYS

10

The Duck Days festival takes place over a long weekend in the middle of February, when birds are migrating.

The event promotes wildlife photography, birdwatching, decoy carving, bird dog training, and waterfowl cooking. Hunting is not part of the official agenda.

Duck Days makes the birds' annual migration through the Delta into a party for people. The ordinary landscape is momentarily transformed: farms and wetlands become festival grounds.

The fast-moving rivers in the Sierra Nevada scour sediment from the mountains, and the slow-moving rivers in the Delta deposit it in the flood plain. Where rivers converge, the natural levees are sometimes close enough to create an area of high ground called a pocket.

There are three pockets in the Delta: one on Roberts Island, one that has been swallowed by Sacramento's suburbs, and one along Cache Slough called Peters Pocket.

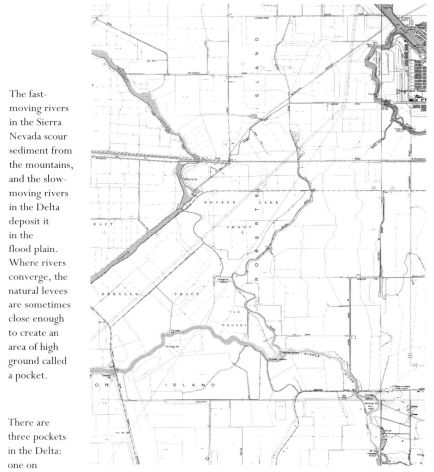

Map 41   156

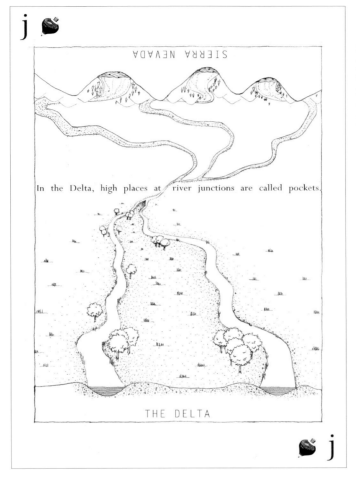

j

SIERRA NEVADA

In the Delta, high places at river junctions are called pockets.

THE DELTA

j

In geology, pocket usually refers to a mineral deposit, like a pocket of ore. In the Delta, the word means a particular kind of landform.

The Delta's pockets are pocket-like in more than one way. They are deposits of alluvial sediment; they are places where things collect; and they are shaped like the front pocket of a pair of pants.

Two worlds
exist at the
same time on
opposite sides
of the Delta's
levees. From
inside the
levee, a
person has no
sense of the
river; from
outside, he has
no sense of the
land.

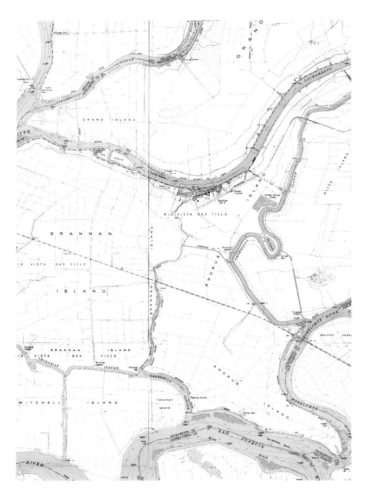

Map 27   158

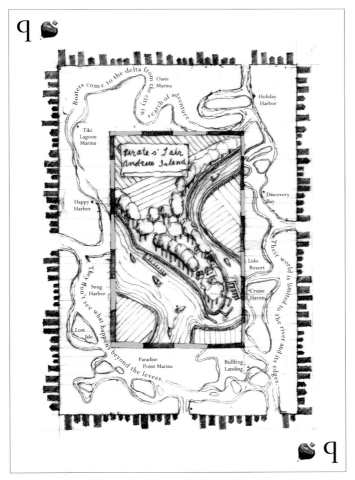

For boaters, the Delta is a playground, a landscape based on a fantasy of adventure. The places they go—marinas, yacht clubs, and hidden docks on channel islands–have evocative, exotic names: Lost Isle, for instance, or Tiki Lagoon, or Pirates' Lair. Their world extends into every corner of the Delta, but only on the water side of the levee.

Worlds collide at the intersection of Fourteenmile Slough (fourteen miles from Stockton) and Disappointment Slough (what befell someone there?). The names give different connotations and associations to places that look the same on the map.

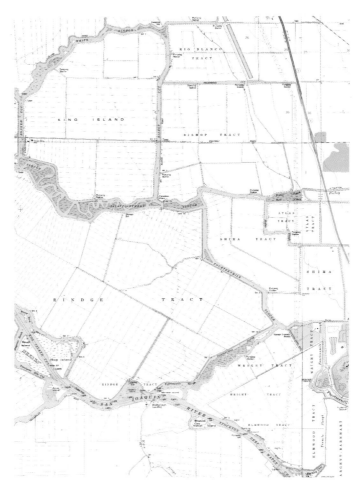

Map 35   160

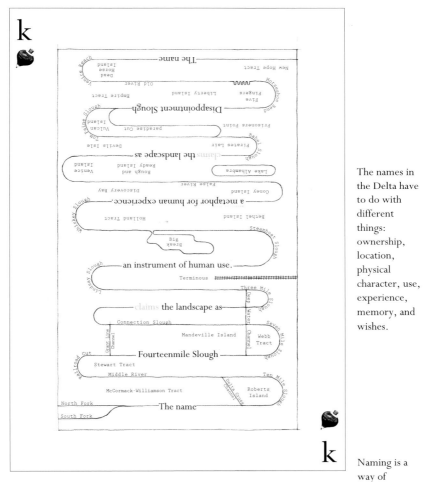

The names in the Delta have to do with different things: ownership, location, physical character, use, experience, memory, and wishes.

Naming is a way of ordering the world. It makes the landscape into a mirror of experience; sometimes it makes places into poetry.

Highway 80, which connects San Francisco and Sacramento, makes one side of a triangle that surrounds the Delta. Like the other two legs, Highway 5 and Highway 580, it has become a corridor for urbanization. Most of this development turns its back on the Delta.

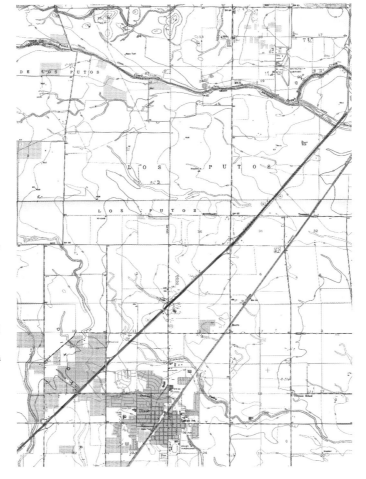

Map 7

162

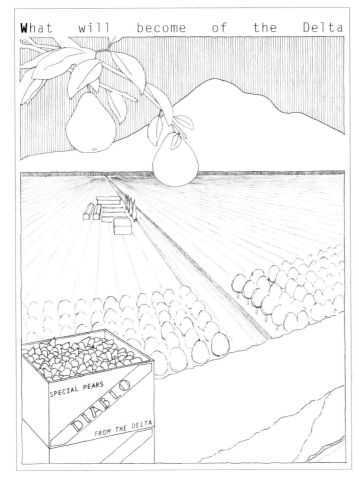

What will become of the Delta

The Delta is at risk because so few people know it. The landscape is almost as foreign to residents of the expanding cities at its edges as it is to water users in faraway Los Angeles.

SPECIAL PEARS

DIABLO

FROM THE DELTA

How can the Delta be made known? Could specialty produce and agricultural tourism create an image of the place for city people?

Highway 5, which was built after the publication of this map, has engendered nearly continuous development along the eastern edge of the Delta.

Lodi's growth is eroding the ring of orchards that used to surround it.

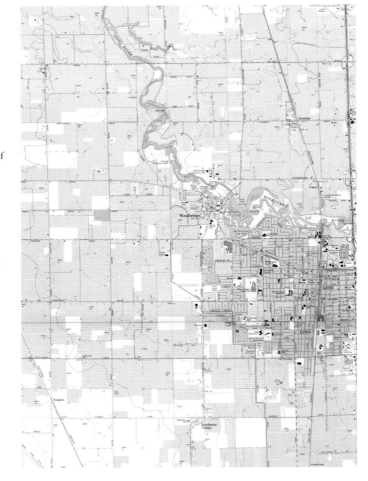

Map 30

164

as conflicting groups negotiate its use

There are many different groups with interests in the Delta, and they all have legitimate claims. One of the most important questions for the future is how to accommodate multiple needs and desires for the landscape.

Lloyd Schmitt's modest little Boxie Boat could inspire a solution to the conflicts that arise between boaters and growers over erosion. It went fast, but it created almost no wake. Voyagers had fun, and the levees that protected farm land were not damaged by waves.

Development has nearly surrounded the Delta, and it is likely to continue. People who live in cities and suburbs almost never have the chance to see herons or orchards: urban growth increases the need for relief from the city.

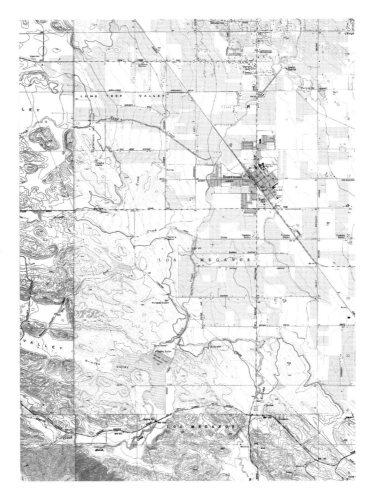

Map 38   166

as different agendas arise and overlap

The Delta could be a respite from the city; people in search of natural or pastoral scenery could go there. A place like the Cosumnes River Preserve or the Yolo Bypass, where habitat and farming mix, could become an oasis for urban refugees.

Water exported from the Delta is pumped up into the Diablo foothills to generate head. From there it flows by gravity through the Great Valley. The State Water Project includes a second set of pumps at the south end of the valley. They send the water over the Tehachapi Mountains to Los Angeles.

The energy required to run the pumps makes the Department of Water Resources the largest consumer of electricity in the state of California.

Map 59 168

as aque**d**ucts take more water to the city?

The Delta is interesting because it is complicated. The water users are its most powerful constituency. If the landscape remains a blank in their minds, how will they understand the value of other people's demands? The greatest threat to the Delta's future is its invisibility.

Notes: Playing Card Map

The Delta, 1869
Map provided by the State Lands Commission, Sacramento, California.

Map 13/Asparagus
In *The Settlement Geography of the Sacramento-San Joaquin Delta, California*, John Thompson says that asparagus was introduced to the Delta in the early 1850s (p. 339); the California Asparagus Commission pinpoints the date at 1852 (http://www.calasparagus.com/industry/background.htm, 5/13/2003). Figures on the number of canneries and their output come from "Chinatowns in the Delta: The Chinese in the Sacramento-San Joaquin Delta, 1870-1960," by George Chu (p. 33).

Map 53/A Farmer's Calendar
Statistics on pear acreage and production were provided by Chris Zanobini of the California Pear Advisory Board, December 1998. Mr. Wong Yow's calendar is reproduced in Peter Leung's *One Day, One Dollar*, pp. 38-39.

Map 48/Fortified New Town
Califia was the queen of the first California, a mythical island paradise described in Garcia Ordonez de Montalvo's 16th-century Spanish romance, *The Adventures of Esplandian*. For the evolution of the new Califia, see John Wildermuth's "Gold Rush or Fool's Gold" and Elizabeth Bell's "Delta's Field of Dreams" in the *San Francisco Chronicle*.

Map 14/Agricultural Zoning
Criteria for opening the Sacramento Weir are from the Department of Water Resource's web site (http://wwwdwr.water.ca.gov/dwrfloodupdate/Media_Sac-weir.html#anchor1251360, 6/2/2000). Information about periods of inundation in the Yolo Bypass from 1934-35 to 1997-98 was provided by the

Delta Protection Commission and can be found through the Yolo Basin Foundation (http://www.yolobasin.org/figures.html, 5/20/03). It was compiled from DWR's stream gaging station, "Yolo Bypass Near Lisbon."

Map 10/Farms Become Suburbs
Statistics on population growth in the Sacramento area are from Fair California (http://www.fairus.org/html/msas/042cascr.htm, 8/11/02). Information on the conversion of farmland to suburbs was provided by the California Department of Conservation, Office of Land Conservation.

Map 3/Beet Harvester
For a history of sugar beets in the Delta, see Thompson, *op. cit.*, pp. 352-357. Lloyd Schmitt described the invention of the harvester in his story "Inventing a Sugar Beet Harvester" in *Schmitty's Short Stories and Poems*, p. 99; other stories in his collections tell about his further adventures with the machine.

Map 26/Dredger
This drawing is based on images and descriptions from Thompson and Dutra, *The Tule Breakers*, a history of the sidedraft clamshell dredger, pp. 102, 114, 221, 276, 285, 312.

Map 6/Joint Operations Control Center
For a beautiful description of the process of releasing water from the dams, see Joan Didion's essay "Holy Water" in *The White Album*.

Map 60/Gulping
This drawing is based on urban and agricultural water use statistics from the Delta Protection Commission's *Background Report on Water Issues* (http://www.delta.ca.gov/bkgrpt.html, 11/16/02).

Map 11/Domestic Water Use

Statistics about average residential water use are documented in the East Bay Municipal Water District's Urban Water Management Plan 2000 (http://www.ebmud.com/water_&_environment/water_supply/urban_water_management_plan/default.htm, 5/20/2003) and in the Delta Protection Commission's *Background Report on Water Issues* (http://www.delta.ca.gov/bkgrpt.html, 11/16/02). Information about outdoor use was provided in an e-mail from Simon Eching, Department of Water Resources, January 2002.

Map 20/Yolo Bypass

Information about flood flows in the bypass and river channel was obtained from the DWR web site (http://wwwdwr.water.ca.gov/dwrfloodupdate/Media_SRFCP-system.html, 6/2/02).

Map 9/Tule Fog

The use of the echo board is described in *King and Queen of the River: The Legendary Paddle-wheel Steamboats Delta King and Delta Queen* by Stan Garvey, p. 41.

Map 17/Whirling Disease

The status of whirling disease in California is summarized in the Whirling Disease Foundation's "State by State Survey of Whirling Disease Information" (http://www.whirling-disease.org/Map/sur-abc.html, 7/11/02).

Map 24/Hydraulic Mining

The mining equipment in this drawing is based on images in two catalogues, "Hydraulic Giants, Manufactured by John Hendy Iron Works," from 1911, and "W. T. Garratt's Brass and Bell Foundry, Machine and Hydraulic Works," from 1883. For a comprehensive description of hydraulic mining and its disastrous consequences, see *Imperial San Francisco: Urban Power, Earthly Ruin* by Gray Brechin, pp. 30-53.

Map 31/Invasive Species

The date of water hyacinth's appearance on the Sacramento is given in "Water Hyacinth in California" (http://homepage.westmont.edu/u/outside/phil.soderman/www/hyacinfo.htm, 11/19/01).

Map 19/Boxie Boat

Lloyd Schmitt describes the history of the Boxie and provides a plan and elevation of the boat in his story "The Boxie Boat" in *Schmitty's Short Stories and Poems*, p. 49.

Map 12/Happy Reading Club

The history of the Happy Reading Club is documented in Peter Leung's *One Day, One Dollar*, pp. 71-72.

Map 21/Ferries

Thompson concludes his discussion of river transportation in the Delta with a summary of conditions at the time of writing, *op. cit.*, p. 413.

Map 22/Casinos Become Museums

The plan of Locke was based in part on a sketch in *Bitter Melon*, Gillenkirk and Motlow, p. 135.

Map 36/The Pleasures of Stockton

The drawings and map of Stockton's sights are based on photographs and addresses in *Stockton Memories*, Wood and Covello, pp. 49, 150, 153, 155.

A

acre-foot/325,851 gallons, the amount of water needed to cover an acre of land with water one foot deep. Two acre-feet per day equal one cubic foot per second. Three acre-feet per day equal one million gallons per day.

Alien Land Law/a 1913 law that prevented Asians from owning agricultural land in California. It was repealed in 1948.

alluvium/the sediment deposited by flowing water.

anadromous/migrating upstream to breed. The anadromous fish in the Delta travel from the ocean upriver to lay their eggs.

aqueduct/Two aqueducts, the California Aqueduct and the Delta-Mendota Canal, carry water from the Delta to southern California. The Mokolumne Aqueducts carry water across the Delta to the East Bay Municipal Utilities District.

aquifer/an underground formation of rock, soil, or sediment that is naturally saturated with water. An aquifer stores groundwater.

asparagus/one of the Delta's main export crops. At one point Isleton was the center of production for 90% of the world's asparagus.

California Aqueduct

B

bascule bridge/a drawbridge counterbalanced so that when one end is lowered the other one rises.

beet harvester/a machine for harvesting beets. The first commercially successful sugar beet harvester, the Marbeet, was invented in the Delta by Lloyd Schmitt during World War II and produced by the Blackwelder Manufacturing Company of Rio Vista.

boil/an eruption of river water that has seeped through or under a levee and risen to the surface of the ground.

borrow pit/a trench or pit dug to acquire material for building levees.

Boxie Boat/a small overnight boat designed by Lloyd Schmitt. It cost very little to manufacture or maintain and generated almost no wake.

bascule bridge

Boxie Boat

Big Break

Caterpillar

Chinatown

cut

brackish/mixed fresh and salt water.

breach/Levee breaches in the Delta are a constant hazard; sometimes they are caused by the deterioration of the levee, and sometimes they are caused by high water. Some levees have been breached repeatedly: McCormack-Williamson Tract, Venice Island, Quimby Island, and Prospect Island have all flooded at least three times since 1930.

break/ a crack that runs all the way through a levee; the location of a breach. Big Break, near Jersey Island, was the result of a levee breach in 1928; a subsided island flooded and was not pumped dry again.

C

CALFED/a consortium of state and Federal agencies brought together to negotiate the future of the Delta.

Caterpillar/a tractor system with continuous chain treads patented by Benjamin Holt in Stockton in 1907. The treads were developed to prevent machinery from sinking into the muddy ground of the Delta.

Central Valley Project/a Federal water project that sends water from the Delta to farmers in the San Joaquin Valley.

channel/1. a natural or artificial waterway that sometimes or always contains moving water or that forms a connecting link between two bodies of water. It has a definite bed and banks that confine the water. 2. the deep portion of a river or stream, where the main current flows.

channel island/an unreclaimed island in the channel of a Delta river.

Chinatown/a Chinese district. Rio Vista, Sacramento, Stockton, Isleton, Walnut Grove, and Courtland all had Chinatowns; Locke was an autonomous Chinese village.

Chinese Exclusion Act/an 1882 act of Congress prohibiting the immigration of Chinese laborers to the United States.

crown/the top of a levee.

cut/a man-made channel dug to straighten the meandering course of a river, to connect two rivers, or to mark a property boundary.

D

Delta Cross Channel/a channel dug as part of the Central Valley Project to move water from the east side of the Delta to the west.

Delta Protection Commission/a California agency chartered by the 1992 Delta Protection Act to represent the interests of the Delta.

Delta smelt/*(Hypomesus transpacificus)* a small, slender fish that lives only in the brackish water of the Delta. It was listed by the federal and California governments as threatened in 1993.

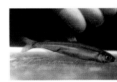

Delta smelt

Department of Water Resources/the agency that manages California's water infrastructure.

distributary/a stream that branches away from the main course of a river and discharges into another body of water.

draft/the depth of a boat's keel below the water line, usually determined when the boat is loaded.

drainage basin/the area drained by a river system. The Delta's drainage basin is the Great Central Valley of California.

draw/to require a specific depth of water for floating.

dredger/a machine for excavating river channels and placing material on levees. Dredgers, especially the side-draft clamshell dredger, were essential to the reclamation of the Delta.

dredger

drought/water shortage. California has a drought ecology. The annual precipitation in Los Angeles is 12.01 inches.

E

echo board/a primitive sonar device used to aid navigation through tule fog.

effluent/the water discharged after use in the treatment of sewage.

encroachment/the advance of uses, plant growth, fill excavation, buildings, permanent structures, or development that may impede or alter the flow capacity of a floodplain.

Endangered Species Act/an act of Congress passed in 1973 to provide the means to protect ecosystems upon which species threatened with extinction depend.

estuary/the part of the wide lower course of a river where its current is met by the tides.

F

fallow

fallowing/a program to generate water by paying farmers to take land out of cultivation. The irrigation water that would have been used is sent instead to urban areas or stored for future use.

farm camp/a settlement for housing agricultural workers and preparing produce for shipment. Delta farm camps, usually located between the rivers and the fields, served historically as entrepot points for goods and meeting places for people.

fetch/the distance over which a wind blows. Light winds can create large waves if their fetch is long; that is why the waves that occur when Delta islands flood have so much erosive power.

fish truck/the tanker truck that carries fish rescued from the aqueducts' pumps back into the Sacramento River.

flood

flood/1. the general and temporary inundation of dry land by overflowing inland or tidal waters. 2. the unusual or rapid accumulation or runoff or surface waters from any source.

flood crest/the maximum elevation reached by the waters of a flood at a given location.

flood plain/1. level land that may be submerged by flood waters. 2. a plain built up by stream deposition.

freeboard/1. the vertical distance between the normal maximum water level and the levee crest. 2. space allowed above the designed water surface level. The Federal Flood Control Project levees were designed to have three feet of freeboard.

G

Gardner, Earle Stanley / the author of the Perry Mason series and a Delta habitué. He wrote several travel books about boating in the Delta.

Great Central Valley / the drainage basin of the Delta. Two thirds of the state of California drain into its major rivers, the Sacramento and the San Joaquin.

groundwater / 1. the water that moves within and under the Delta's porous soils. 2. water that is percolated into natural underground aquifers.

gulping / the pumping protocol that sends water to the aqueducts at high tide and not at low tide. It minimizes the effects of pumping on water conditions in the Delta.

Great Central Valley

H

hundred-year flood / a flood of a magnitude that has a one in one hundred chance of occurring in any given year. Also called a base flood.

I

infrastructure / the engineered structures that underlie inhabitation. The levees constitute infrastructure that supports the Delta; the Delta is infrastructure that supports Los Angeles.

island / pieces of land bounded on all sides by rivers. Islands in the Delta define ownership; they dictate the organization of reclamation districts; and they make it difficult to cross the region in a straight line.

island

J

Joint Operations Control Office/operations center for the State and Federal water projects. Water is routed by the Operations Control Office from the dams, through the Delta, and to the pumps.

K

Kuomintang

kitchen garden/a garden where fruit and vegetables are grown for consumption by members of a household.
Kuomintang/the Chinese Nationalist Party. It had branches in Courtland's Chinatown and in Locke.

L

Legal Delta/the boundary of the Delta defined by the Delta Protection Act of 1959.
levee/an embankment built along the banks of a river or stream to protect land from inundation or to confine the stream's flow to a fixed channel.

M

meander

meander/a back-and-forth bend produced by a river's erosion and deposition of material along its banks.
mean sea level/the mean level halfway between high and low tides. It is used as a datum in surveying land elevations and sea depths.
Metropolitan Water District/a consortium of 26 cities and water districts that provides water to nearly 17 million people in Southern California.

mitigation/the amelioration of the adverse environmental impacts of an activity.

N

night boat/the passenger boat that traveled overnight between Sacramento and San Francisco. Night boats were in service until the start of World War II.

non-project levee/a levee maintained by private owners or a reclamation district. There are no design standards for non-project levees.

night boat

O

oxbow lake/a lake formed when a meander bend of a river is cut off from the main channel.

oxidation/the combination of a substance with oxygen. The organic material in the Delta's peat soils oxidizes when it is exposed to air, and the soil disappears.

pear

P

pear/*(Pyrus communis)* the main tree crop in the Delta.

Pacific Flyway/a route along the Pacific coast taken by migrating birds. The Delta is an important stopping point between breeding grounds in the north and wintering grounds in the south.

peat/soil that consists mainly of decomposed or decomposing plant material. Most of the Delta is peat.

piping/the passage of water through tiny apertures in a levee. As the water travels, it erodes the apertures and makes them bigger; eventually it carries soil from the levee to the inside of the island.

Pacific Flyway

pocket

pocket/an area of high ground created by the natural levees of diverging streams.

project levee/a levee funded by the Federal government. The design standard for project levees is the hundred-year flood.

pump/1. a machine for raising the level of water. 2. to lift water or make it flow by using a pump.

Q

R

reach/a length, distance, or leg of a river channel.

reclamation/making land arable. In the Delta, reclamation meant draining the swamps.

restoration/the reconstitution of an original condition. The restoration of the Delta's original circumstances is impossible.

revetment/a stone, concrete, or sandbag facing that prevents the erosion of an earthen bank.

riparian/relating to the banks or course of a river or stream.

riprap/broken stones or cobbles used to reinforce the water side of a levee.

river mile/a river distance measured along the thalweg.

row crop/crops sown, cultivated, and harvested in rows, like corn, wheat, potatoes, beets, or asparagus.

riprap

row crop

S

salinity/the level of dissolved salts in water. In the Delta, this depends on the amount of fresh water flowing through the rivers to the ocean.

sandbag chimney/a cylinder of sandbags around a boil that prevents it from growing. The water in the boil rises to the height of the sandbag chimney rather than migrating through the soil.

Schmitt, Lloyd / the inventor of the Marbeet beet harvester and the Boxie Boat. He was a native of Rio Vista.

scour / the removal of soil or sediment by moving water.

sedimentation / the deposition of material being carried by a river. The slower water moves, the more sediment it deposits.

Shima, Togo / the Potato King. A Japanese-American farmer who cultivated land on Webb Tract and Bacon Island in the first part of the 20th century.

ship channel / a deep water channel dredged to allow access to inland ports by ocean-going vessels. One of the Delta's ship channels goes to Stockton, the other to Sacramento.

Stockton Deep
Water Channel

shipwreck / More than 100 ships have been wrecked between Sacramento and Sherman Island. Some have been raised; others remain on the bottom.

sipping / a pumping protocol that exports more water from the Delta at high tide than at low tide.

slough / a side channel or inlet from a river. Water in a slough can flow in either direction depending on the tide.

sluice-box / a wooden box through which gold-laden water was run by hydraulic miners. The gold settled to the bottom of the box and the water and the lighter sediment washed through.

spillway / an overflow channel for flood water.

State Water Project / the infrastructure built by the state to supply cities in Southern California with drinking water.

striped bass / (*Morone saxatilis*) a fish species introduced to the Delta in the 19th century for commercial fishing. Prolific and competitive, the striped bass have become predators of native Delta species.

striped bass

subsidence / the falling of land elevations because of oxidation.

sugar beet / (*Beta vulgaris*) a beet cultivar from whose roots sugar can be extracted. Sugar beets were one of the Delta's primary crops from the 1920s through the 1950s.

surge / a swelling, rolling, forward-sweeping series of large waves or billows that results in elevated water levels.

sugar beet

swamp / 1. a bottomland that floods seasonally. 2. a lowland saturated with water. Swampy landscapes have been seen historically as pestilential, dangerous, and without value.

Swamp and Overflowed Lands Act/an act of Congress passed in 1850. It made marshlands available for settlement on the condition that they were reclaimed for agriculture.

swing bridge/a drawbridge that opens by swinging sideways about a turntable.

California
Least Tern

endangered

T

thalweg/the line that runs along the deepest part of a river channel.

threatened and endangered/categories defined by the Endangered Species Act. Endangered species face extinction; threatened species are likely to become endangered in the foreseeable future unless action is taken.

tide/the periodic variation in the level of oceans, bays, gulfs, and estuaries caused by the gravitational pull of the sun and moon.

toe/1. the line where the slope of a levee intersects the ground plane. 2. the downstream edge at the base of a dam.

tree crop/crops grown, cultivated, and harvested on trees. Pears are the main tree crop in the Delta.

tributary/a stream or river that flows into another river or body of water.

tule/*(Scirpus acutus)* a rush-like plant native to the Delta.

tule fog/ground fog.

tule

U

underground gas storage/storage of natural gas extracted from and brought to the Delta. The biggest fields are near Rio Vista and on Twitchell, Andrus, and Tyler Islands.

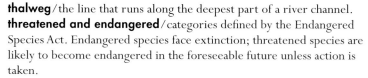

V

vertical-lift bridge/a drawbridge that operates by counterweights housed in towers. The counterweights are the exact weight of the lift span.

W

wake/turbulence left by a boat moving through water. Wakes in the Delta erode levees.

water agency/one of three Delta agencies representing local interests in water quality negotiations.

water export/the transport of water out of the Delta for agricultural and urban uses in the San Joaquin Valley and Southern California.

water hyacinth/ *(Eichhornia crassipes)* an invasive plant, introduced to the Delta after the turn of the 20th century, that chokes rivers and sloughs.

water rights/the right to use water from a particular source. California recognizes different rights to water: riparian right, the right based on the ownership of property that abuts a water course; appropriative right, the entitlement based on the actual use of the water; and pueblo right, the entitlement granted under Spanish and Mexican law to a town to use adjacent water sources to meet its needs.

watershed /the whole surface area that drains into a river or lake.

wetland/a piece of land characterized by frequent inundation and water-tolerant plants and animals. Wetlands are protected by the Clean Water Act. Their legal definition varies: the Army Corps of Engineers defines them as "areas that are inundated or saturated by surface water or groundwater at a frequency and duration sufficient to support, and that normal circumstances do support, a prevalence of vegetation typically adapted for life in saturated soil conditions. Wetlands generally include swamps, marshes, bogs, and similar areas."

water hyacinth

weir

Wong Yow

weir / a structure or barrier that can be moved vertically to divert or raise the water in a river.

winter-run salmon / (*Oncorhynchus tshawytscha*) an anadromous fish native to the Delta and listed by the State of California and the Federal government as endangered.

Wong Yow / an orchard worker, gardener, and handyman who lived in Locke and worked on a ranch near Walnut Grove.

X

X-2 line / the line where fresh water meets salt water in the Delta. The location of the line depends on how much water is flowing to the ocean, or, differently said, on how much water is being sent to the aqueducts.

Y

Yolo Bypass / a spillway that carries up to five sixths of the water from the Sacramento River during floods. The legislation creating the bypass stipulated that only crops that would bend during flood flows could be planted there.

Z

Bibliography and Other Sources

The *Delta Primer* is based in part on the publications cited in this bibliography and in part on other sources: conversations with **Margit Aramburu**, Delta Protection Commission, Walnut Grove (1996-2002); **Malcolm McCormack**, Walnut Grove (1996-2002); **Kyser Shimasaki**, Bacon Island (1997-2002); **Eleanor Fong**, Tyler Island (1997-1999); **Lloyd Schmitt**, Rio Vista (1997-1999); **Chris Zanobini**, California Pear Advisory Board, Sacramento (1998); **Stein Buer**, Department of Water Resources, Sacramento (1997); **Earle Cooley**, Medford Island (1997); **George Fong**, Tyler Island(1997); **Alex Hildebrand**, Manteca (1997); **Dante Nomellini**, Stockton (1997); **Hal Schell**, Stockton (1997); **Jim and Sally Shanks**, Staten Island (1997); **Bill Shelton**, Walnut Grove (1997); **John Winther**, Lafayette (1997); and the staff of the **Fish Protective Facility** (1997); the **United States Geological Survey** 7.5 minute series map quadrangles that comprise the Delta; public meetings of the **CALFED Bay-Delta Program** (1997-1999) and the **Delta Protection Commission** (1997-2001); and **direct observation** of the landscape from 1996 to 2002.

Sources in Print:

Abel, Heather, "Water Wars," *San Francisco Bay Guardian*, January 20, 1999: 23-28.

Alsop, Fred J. III, *Birds of North America, Eastern Region*, New York: DK Publishing, Inc., 2001.

Background Information: The Delta Wetlands Reservoir and Wildlife Habitat and excerpts from the Delta Wetlands EIS/EIR, provided by Delta Wetlands, Lafayette, California, 1996.

Barth, Dianne, "Turning islands into water banks," *The Record*, August 3, 1997: A1.

Beiser, Vince, "California to spend $1 billion for biggest environmental restoration in U.S. history," *The Oakland Tribune*, October 5, 1997: A1.

———, "Smaller Peripheral Canal proposal raises its head," *The Oakland Tribune*, October 5, 1997: A18.

Bell, Elizabeth, "Delta's Field of Dreams," *San Francisco Chronicle*, July 18, 2000: A1.

Bowie, Aug. J., Jr., *A Practical Treatise on Hydraulic Mining in California*, New York: D. Van Nostrand, Publisher, 1885.

Bowman, Catherine, Erin Hallissy, and Edward W. Lempinen, "Wind, levee breaks still pose threats," *San Francisco Chronicle*, January 7, 1997: A1.

Brechin, Gray, *Imperial San Francisco: Urban Power, Earthly Ruin*, Berkeley: University of California Press, 1999.

CALFED Bay-Delta Program, *Ecosystem Restoration Program Plan, Executive Summary and Volumes 1 and 2*, photocopied report booklets distributed by CALFED, 1999.

———, *Implementation Plan: Draft Programmatic EIS/EIR Technical Appendix*, photocopied report booklets distributed by CALFED, 1999.

———, *Levee System Integrity Program Plan: Draft Programmatic EIS/EIR Technical Appendix*, photocopied report booklets distributed by CALFED, 1999.

———, *Programmatic EIS/EIR, Executive Summary and Technical Appendix*, photocopied report booklets distributed by CALFED, 1998.

———, *Science in Action: News from the CALFED Bay-Delta Science Program*, December 2001.

CALFED Levees and Channels Technical Team and Seismic Vulnerability Sub-Team, *Seismic Vulnerability of the Sacramento-San Joaquin Delta Levees*, photocopied report booklets distributed by CALFED, 2000.

CALFED Storage and Conveyance Refinement

Team, *Preliminary Working Draft: CALFED Bay-Delta Program Storage and Conveyance Component Inventories*, photocopied report booklets distributed by CALFED, 1997.

California Duck Days 1998 At A Glance, brochure distributed by California Duck Days, 1998.

The California Water Plan Update, Bulletin 160-98, Sacramento: Department of Water Resources, 1998.

Castle, Allen, "Locke: A Chinese Chinatown," *The Pacific Historian*, Vol. 24, No. 1, Spring 1980, pp. 1-7.

Chu, George, "Chinatowns in the Delta: The Chinese in the Sacramento-San Joaquin Delta, 1870-1960," *The California Historical Society Quarterly*, Vol. XLIX, No. 1, March 1970, pp. 21-37.

The Cosumnes River Preserve: Partnering with Agriculture for Habitat Protection and Compatible Economic Development, 2000. Copy provided by Valerie Calegari, Cosumnes River Preserve.

Cosumnes River Preserve: Take a walk on the wild side, brochure distributed by the Nature Conservancy of California, 1998.

Cosumnes River Preserve: Willow Slough Nature Trail, brochure distributed by the Nature Conservancy of California, 1994.

D'Allemagne, Henry René, *Antique Playing Cards: A Pictorial Treasury* (Carol Belanger Grafton, ed.), Mineola, N.Y.: Dover Publications, 1996.

Dawson, Robert and Gray Brechin, *Farewell, Promised Land: Waking from the California Dream*, Berkeley: University of California Press, 1999.

Delta-Estuary, California's Inland Coast: A Public Trust Report, Sacramento: California State Lands Commission, 1991.

Delta Farmland Under Siege as Developers Move In, *San Francisco Chronicle: Sunday*, August 10, 1997: 1.

Department of Conservation, Office of Land Conservation, "1984-2000 Land Use Conversion Tables, Contra Costa, Sacramento, San Joaquin, Solano, and Yolo Counties," transmitted by facsimile by the Division of Land Resource Protection, 3/18/02.

Diderot, Denis, *A Diderot Pictorial Encyclopedia of Trades and Industry, Volume One*, (Charles C. Gillispie, ed.) Mineola, N.Y.: Dover Publications, Inc., 1959.

Didion, Joan, *The White Album*, New York: Simon and Schuster, 1979.

Dutra, Edward, "History of Sidedraft Clamshell Dredging in California," 1976. Brochure distributed by the Dutra Dredging Company, Rio Vista, California.

The Dutra Museum of Dredging, brochure distributed by the Dutra Dredging Company, Rio Vista, California.

Eaton, Michael R., "Restoration of Natural Processes on the Cosumnes River Preserve: Overview and Status Report," 1998. Copy provided by Valerie Calegarie, Cosumnes River Preserve.

Ecosystem Restoration Program Plan, Draft Volumes 1 and 2, Sacramento: CALFED Bay-Delta Program, 1999.

A Field Checklist for Birds of the Cosumnes River Preserve, brochure distributed by the Nature Conservancy of California, 1996.

First Beet Harvester (exhibit), catalog no. 91-836-1, Rio Vista Museum, 16 N. Front Street, Rio Vista, CA 94571.

Garvey, Stan, *King and Queen of the River: The legendary paddle-wheel steamboats Delta King and Delta Queen*, Menlo Park: River Heritage Press, 1999.

Gillenkirk, Jeff and James Motlow, *Bitter Melon: Inside America's Last Rural Chinatown*, Berkeley: Heyday Books, 1987.

Hal Schell's Delta Map and Guide, Stockton: Schell Books, no date.

Harter, Jim, ed., *Animals: 1419 Copyright-Free Illustrations of Mammals, Birds, Fish, Insects, etc.*, Mineola, N.Y.: Dover Publications, Inc., 1979.

Hydraulic Giants, Manufactured by John Hendy Iron Works, San Francisco, Cal. U.S.A., catalogue, 1911.

Hundley, Norris, Jr., *The Great Thirst: Californians and Water: A History*, Berkeley: University of California Press, 2001.

Johnson, Stephen, Gerald Haslam, and Robert Dawson, *The Great Central Valley: California's Heartland*, Berkeley: University of California Press, 1993.

Kahrl, William L., ed., *The California Water Atlas*, Sacramento: The Governor's Office of Planning and Research, 1979; distributed by William Kaufmann, Los Altos, CA.

Kelley, Robert, *Battling the Inland Sea*, Berkeley: University of California Press, 1989.

———, *Gold vs. grain: the hydraulic mining controversy in California's Sacramento Valley ; a chapter in the decline of the concept of laissez faire*, Glendale, Calif.: A. H. Clark Co., 1959.

Land Location and Boundary Section, California State Lands Commission, *A Map and Record Investigation of Historical Sites and Shipwrecks Along the Sacramento River Between Sacramento City and Sherman Island*, Sacramento: State of California, 1988.

Land Subsidence: A Threat to California's Delta, brochure distributed by the USDA Soil Conservation Service, 1990.

Land Use and Resource Management Plan for the Primary Zone of the Delta, Walnut Grove: Delta Protection Commission, 1995.

Lathrop is a safer place thanks to Califia gift, *Lathrop Rush*, Issue 2, July 1998, p. 1.

Leung, Peter C. Y., *One Day, One Dollar: The Chinese Farming Experience in the Sacramento River Delta, California*, Taipei: The Liberal Arts Press, 1994.

Lindelof, Bill, "County acts on plan to save Locke," *The Sacramento Bee*, August 31, 2000: B1.

Lucas, Greg, "Bay-Delta Water Pact Has Option for Canal," *San Francisco Chronicle*, June 9, 2000: A3.

MacMullen, Jerry, *Paddlewheel Days in California*, Stanford: Stanford University Press, 1944.

Making the Delta Bloom: Creation of the Delta Farms, two brochures published by the Angel Island Institute of California, 1992, and distributed by the Catherine Coffin Phillips Library, Tiburon, CA.

Martin, Glen, "Divvying Up Our Water," *San Francisco Chronicle*, June 25, 1999: A1.

———, "Reclaiming a River," *San Francisco Chronicle*, February 22, 2000: A1.

McPeak, Sunne Wright, "Protecting the New Mother Lode," *San Francisco Chronicle*, August 1, 1997, p. A27.

Minick, Roger and Dave Bohn, *Delta West: The Land and People of the Sacramento-San Joaquin Delta*, Berkeley: Scrimshaw Press, 1969.

Moreland, Carl and David Bannister, *Antique Maps*, London: Phaidon Press, 1993.

Minton, Torri, "Sacramento River Covers Island Resort," *San Francisco Chronicle*, January 7, 1997: A13.

Payne, Walter A., ed., *Benjamin Holt: The Story of the Caterpillar Tractor*, Stockton: University of the Pacific, 1982.

Peterson, Roger Tory, *Western Birds*, Boston and New York: Houghton Mifflin Company, 1990.

Reisner, Marc, *Cadillac Desert: The American West and Its Disappearing Water*, New York: Penguin Books, 1993.

———, "A Tale of Delta Quakes and Levees," *Los Angeles Times*, January 19, 1997: M1.

The Resources Agency, Department of Water Resources, *Alternatives for Delta Water Transfer*, Sacramento: State of California, 1983.

The Resources Agency, Department of Water Resources, "Delta Subsidence Investigation: Progress Report for Fiscal Years 1986-87 and 1987-88." Photocopied report booklets distributed by the Resources Agency, 1989.

The Resources Agency of California, *Governor's Flood Emergency Action Team: Preliminary Report*. Photocopied report booklets distributed by the Resources Agency, 1997.

Russle, Sabin, "In Flood's Wake, Worries Grow About Health Hazards," *San Francisco Chronicle*, January 7, 1997: A13.

Sacramento-San Joaquin Delta Atlas, Sacramento: California Department of Water Resources, 1995.

Schell, Hal, *Dawdling on the Delta*, Stockton: Schell Books, 1979.

Schenker, Heath, ed., *Picturing California's Other Landscape: The Great Central Valley*, Berkeley: Heyday Books, 1999.

Schmitt, Lloyd, *The Best of Schmitty's Short Stories*, Raleigh: Pentland Press, 1999.

———, *Rio Vista Short Stories*, Bend: Maverick Publications, Inc., 1991.

———, *Schmitty's Short Stories and Poems, Volume I*, Detroit: Harlo Press, 1986.

———, *Schmitty's Short Stories and Poems, Volume II*, Detroit: Harlo Press, 1987.

Schreiber, Lady Charlotte, *Playing Cards of various Ages and Countries: Selected from the Collection of Lady Charlotte Schreiber, Volume I. English, Scottish, Dutch and Flemish*, London: John Murray, 1892.

———, *Playing Cards of various Ages and Countries: Selected from the Collection of Lady Charlotte Schreiber, Volume II. French and German*, London: John Murray, 1893.

———, *Playing Cards of various Ages and Countries: Selected from the Collection of Lady Charlotte Schreiber, Volume III. Swiss, Swedish, Russian, Polish, Italian, Spanish and Portuguese, with a supplement of other countries*, London: John Murray, 1895.

State Water Resources Control Board, *Water Right Decision 1485*, Sacramento: State of California, 1978.

Thompson, John, *The Settlement Geography of the Sacramento-San Joaquin Delta, California*, doctoral dissertation, Stanford University, 1958. Distributed by UMI Dissertation Services, Ann Arbor, Michigan.

Thompson, John and Edward A. Dutra, *The Tule Breakers: The Story of the California Dredge*, Stockton: The Stockton Corral of Westerners / University of the Pacific, 1983.

Tucker, E. E., *Field Notes of Reclamation, State Engineer Department*, 1879, photocopy provided by the California State Lands Commission.

Turner, Jerry L. and D. W. Kelley, *Fish Bulletin 136: Ecological Studies of the Sacramento-San Joaquin Delta, Part II, Fishes of the Delta*, Sacramento: State of California, The Resources Agency, Department of Fish and Game, 1966.

United States Department of Agriculture, Soil

Conservation Service, in cooperation with the Regents of the University of California (Agricultural Experiment Station), *Soil Survey of Sacramento County, California*, 1993.

———, in cooperation with the Regents of the University of California (Agricultural Experiment Station) and the California Department of Conservation, *Soil Survey of San Joaquin County, California*, 1992.

———, in cooperation with University of California Agricultural Experiment Station, *Soil Survey of Contra Costa County, California*, 1975.

———, in cooperation with University of California Agricultural Experiment Station, *Soil Survey of Solano County, California*, 1977.

———, in cooperation with University of California Agricultural Experiment Station, *Soil Survey of Yolo County, California*, 1972, reprinted August 1990.

W. T. Garratt's Brass and Bell Foundry, Machine and Hydraulic Works, Manufacturer and Importer of Brass and Iron Goods of Every Variety, for Water Works, Steamships, Rail Roads, Mines, Mills and Plumbers' Work. Steam and Hand Pumps, Iron Pipe and Fittings, catalogue, San Francisco, 1883.

Wildermuth, John, "Gold Rush or Fool's Gold," *San Francisco Chronicle: Sunday*, August 10, 1997: 1

Wolff, Jane, "Rising Water, Falling Land," *ArcCA: Architecture California*, Vol. 1, No. 4, pp. 10-13.

Wood, R. Coke and Leonard Covello, *Stockton Memories: A Pictorial History of Stockton, California*, Fresno: Valley Publishers, 1977.

Zamora, Jim Herron, Ray Delgado, and Eric Brazil, "Threat to levees persists," *San Francisco Examiner*, January 7, 1997: A1.

Electronic Sources:

Alluvium, from *The Hutchison Family Encyclopedia*, http://ebooks.whsmithonline.co.uk/encyclopedia/12/M0035012.htm, 12/19/01.

Bacon Island Bridge, photograph, http://www.californiadelta.org/bacbrge.jpg, 7/16/01.

Bay-Delta Advisory Council (BDAC) Members, http://calfed.ca.gov/ARchives/GeneralArchive/BDACMembers.shtml, 5/13/03

Borealforest.org: Glossaries and Explanations, http://www.borealforest.org/greenspaces.glossary.htm, 12/19/01.

Burton, J., M. Farrell, F. Lord, and R. Lord, "Confinement and Ethnicity: An Overview of World War II Japanese American Relocation Sites," http://www.cr.nps.gov/history/online_books/anthropology74/ce3.htm, 6/29/02.

California Bay-Delta Authority: Glossary of Acronyms, http://calfed.ca.gov/AboutCalfed/GlossaryofAcronyms.shtml, 5/13/03.

California Bay-Delta Authority: Policy Group Members—CALFED Program Structure, http://calfed.ca.gov/AboutCalfed/PolicyGroupMembers.shtml, 5/13/03.

California Bay-Delta Program: California Bay Delta Public Advisory Committee, http://www.calfed.water.ca.gov/bdpac/BDPAC_Members.html, 2/24/02.

CalFed strives to protect remaining In-channel Islands in the Delta, http://www.dfg.ca.gov/news/news00/r2 00 06.html, 3/17/02.

California Asparagus, http://www.calasparagus.com/industry/background.htm, 5/13/03.

California Department of Water Resources, Division of Operations and Maintenance,

Operations Control Office, http://wwwoco.
water.ca.gov/info/about.oco.html, 3/18/02.

California Department of Water Resources:
Glossary, http://wwwdwr.water.ca.gov/
dwrfloodupdate/Media_glossary.html,
6/2/00.

California Department of Water Resources:
Sacramento River Flood Control System, http://
wwwdwr.water.ca.gov/dwrfloodupdate/
Media_SRFCP-system.html, 6/2/02.

California Department of Water Resources:
The Sacramento Weir, http://wwwdwr.
water.ca.gov/dwrfloodupdate/Media_Sac-
weir.html#anchor1251360, 6/2/00.

California Department of Water Resources: State
Water Project, http://wwwdwr.water.ca.gov/
dir-state water projectR2/default.html,
5/4/02.

California Duck Days, http://www.
duckdays.org, 1/15/02.

California Farmland Conversion Report 1996-
98, http://www/consrv.ca.gov/dlrp/fmmp/
fmmp 98rpt.htm, 3/7/02.

California Striped Bass Association, http://
www/fishing-boating.com/csba/, 7/12/02.

California Wetlands Information System: Defining
Wetlands, http://ceres.ca.gov/wetlands/
introduction/defining_wetlands.html, 7/8/02.

The Central Valley Project: It's About Water,
http://www.mp.usbr.gov/cvp/, 5/4/02.

The Challenge of Whirling Disease, http://
www.whirling-disease.org/whirling/
disease.html, 1/23/01.

Commonly Asked Questions About the CALFED
Bay-Delta Program, http://calfed.ca.gov/pub_
info_materials/new_q&a.html, 6/30/99.

Complexity in Meandering Streams, http://
www.susqu.edu/facstaff/b/brakke/
complexity/mcintyre/streams.htm, 12/19/01.

Cosumnes River Preserve, http://www.
cosumnes.org/, 7/2/02.

Cox, William, "RE:," e-mail to Jane Wolff from
WTCOX@dfg.ca.gov concerning whirling
disease in California, 7/22/02.

Delta Protection Commission, Background Report
on Water Issues, http://www.delta.ca.gov/
bkgrpt.html, 11/16/02.

Delta Smelt, http://www.delta.dfg.ca.gov/
gallery/dsmelt.html, 6/30/02.

Department of the Interior/Bureau of
Reclamation Mid-Pacific Region, http://www.
mp.usbr.gov/f_banner.html, 5/13/03.

East Bay Municipal Utilities District, Urban Water
Management Plan 2000, http://www.
ebmud.com/water_&_environment/water_
supply/urban_water_management_plan/
default.htm, 5/20/03.

Eching, Simon, "RE: Question," e-mail to Jane
Wolff from seching@water.ca.gov, 1/4/02.

Fair California, http://www.fairus.org/html/
msas/042cascr.htm, 8/11/02.

Feldheim, Cliff, "California: Winter host for
the Pacific Flyway," http://www.dfg.ca.gov/
coned/ocal/j_a4_5.pdf, 5/5/02.

Ferries of the California Delta, http://www.
californiadelta.org/ferries.htm, 7/16/01.

Flood plain, from The Hutchison
Family Encyclopedia, http://ebooks/
whsmithonline.co.uk/encyclopedia/25/
M0028525.htm, 12/19/01.

Formation of an oxbow lake, http://www.
kented.org.uk/ngfl/rivers/Worksheets1/
worksheet26.htm, 12/19/01.

Frequently Asked Questions, http://www.
whirling-disease.org/whirling/FAQ.html,
1/23/01.

Groundwater: our hidden asset, http://www.
nwl.ac.uk/gwf/gwfimg1.htm, 2/16/02.

A histological section of cartilage from a fish infected with whirling disease...; two 'spores' of Myxobolus..., http://www.bioscio.ohio-state.edu/~parasite/myxobolus.html, 5/15/02.

A History of Chinese Americans in California: Historic Sites—Locke, http://www.ohp.parks.ca.gov/5Views/5Views3h52.htm, 7/12/02.

Lentz, Dave, "Whirling Disease–An Update," http://www.dfg.ca.gov/fishing/wtp/newsletter/fall95.htm, 7/11/02.

Life Cycle of Whirling Disease, http://www.gmfsh.state.nm.us/PageMill_TExt/Fishing/whirlingcycle.html, 8/8/00.

Meander, from The Hutchison Family Encyclopedia, http://ebooks.whsmithonline.co.uk/encyclopedia/48/M0007748.htm, 12/19/01.

Meander Formation and Features of Meandering Streams, http://www.uta.edu/geology/geol1425earth_system/images/gaia_chapter_12/meander_formation.htm, 12/19/01.

Metropolitan Water District of Southern California: Glossary of Water Terms, http://www.mwd.dst.ca.us/mwdh2o/pages/yourwater/glossary/glossary01.html, 6/30/02.

NEBRASKAgriculture in the Classroom: Sugar Beets, http://www.fb.com/nefb/ag-ed/beets.html, 4/14/02.

Niman, Marti, "Whirling Disease's spore-worm-trout cycle now a challenge for New Mexico fisheries," http://www.gmfsh.state.nm.us/PageMill_TExt/Fishing/whirling/html, 1/23/01.

Nonindigenous Aquatic and Semi-aquatic Plants in Freshwater Systems, http://aquat1.ifas.ufl.edu/mcplnt1g.html, 11/19/01.

North American Migration Flyways, http://www.birdnature.com/flyways.html, 5/5/02.

Oxbow lake, from The Hutchison Family Encyclopedia, http://ebooks.whsmithonline.co.uk/encyclopedia/81/P0001981.htm, 12/19/01.

Oxbow lake, http://www/kented.org.uk/ngfl/rivers/River9620Articles/oxbowlake.htm, 12/19/01.

Palmer, Tom, "The War on Whirling Disease," http://www.montana.edu/wwwrc/docs/whirling/centerpage/waron.html, 4/16/02.

Peatlands and Peat, http://www.peatsociety.fi/peatlnd/pleatnland.htm, 7/1/02.

Periods of Yolo Bypass Inundation at Lisbon Gage, 1935-1999, http://www.yolobasin.org/figures.html, 5/20/03; distributed by the Delta Protection Commission, March 2000.

Pettley, John, "The Mt. Diablo Initial Point, Its History and Use," http://www.mdia.org/mdiaipt.htm, 7/25/02.

——, "Mount Diablo Survey Point Establishes Property Boundaries in California and Nevada," http://www.mdshs.org/article.html, 7/25/02.

River, from The Hutchison Family Encyclopedia, http://ebooks.whsmithonline.co.uk/encyclopedia/75/M0007775.htm, 12/19/01.

Scheibe, John, "Cal-Fed scuttles canal plans," www.thereporter.com/Current/News/98/06/daily062498.html, 3/18/02.

Sommer, Ted, Bill Harrell, Matt Nobriga, Randall Brown, Peter Moyle, Wim Kimmerer, and Larry Schemel, "California's Yolo Bypass: Evidence that flood control can be compatible with fisheries, wetlands, wildlife, and agriculture," http://www.fisheries.org;fisheries;F0108/

F0801p6-16.PDF, 7/12/02.

State by State Survey of Whirling Disease Information, http://www.whirling-disease.org/Map/sur-abc.html, 7/11/02.

Reeds, Tules, Cattails, http://www.libarts.wsu.edu/anthro/museum/jm/current/virtual%20exhibits/tules/tulethemes.htm, 11/19/01.

Township and Range: The United States Public Lands Survey, http://geography.about.com/library/weekly/aa090897.htm, 5/17/02.

Water Hyacinth in California, http://homepage.westmont.edu/u/outside/phil.soderman/www/hyacinfo.htm, 11/19/01.

Whirling Disease (Myxobolus cerebralis), http://www.state.me.us/ifw/fish/fishlab/issue2.htm, 4/15/02.

Wisconsin Trout Vulnerable to Whirling Disease, Researcher Says, http://www.seagrant.wisc.edu/Communications/news releases/2002/WhirlingDisease.html, 4/15/02.

Credits

Text/Jane Wolff
Drawings/Jane Wolff and Thomas Hansen
Photographs 1-7, 9-11, frontispiece/Jane Wolff
Photograph 8/Thomas Hansen
Maps/United States Geological Survey
Book design/Jane Wolff, Thomas Hansen, and Sarah Granatir
Conceptual design of the playing card map/Jane Wolff and
John Bass. The drawings *Kitchen Garden*, *Cantina*, and *Moving
the Headquarters* are based on *Three Farm Camps Remembered* by
Jane Wolff and John Bass, ©1997.
Readers/Margit Aramburu, Ken Botnick, Paul Groth,
Elizabeth Meyer, William Morrish, Charles Waldheim, and
Phil Williams
Research assistant/Sarah Van Laanen
Publishing assistant/Taylor Jacobson
Digital technology consultant/David Miller
Fiscal agent/Planet Drum Foundation
Vocabulary images/*California Aqueduct:* California Water
Plan Update Bulletin 160-98, facing p. 3-1; *Big Break:* USGS;
Chinatown: Castle, p. 6; *cut:* Wood and Covello, p. 20; *Delta
smelt:* California Water Plan Update Bulletin 160-98,
p. 4-45; *dredger:* Thompson and Dutra, p. 285; *flood:* California
Water Plan Update Bulletin 160-98, p. 8-12; *island:* USGS;
Kuomintang: Gillenkirk and Motlow, p. 37; *meander:* California
Water Plan Update Bulletin 160-98, p. 4-45; *night boat:*
Garvey, cover; *Pacific Flyway:* California Water Plan Update
Bulletin 160-98, p. 4-47; *row crop:* Wood and Covello, p. 94;
weir: California Water Plan Update Bulletin 160-98, p. 8-13;
Wong Yow: Leung, p. 95; *all other vocabulary illustrations:* Jane
Wolff and Thomas Hansen. Every reasonable effort has been
made to identify owners of copyrights. Errors or omissions
will be corrected in subsequent editions.

Publisher's note

This book and deck of cards make a powerful case for
preserving this beautiful area, the California Delta.
William Stout
San Francisco, California